THE GOLDEN LAMB
Tales from the
INNSIDE

Fred Compton

ORANGE*frazer*PRESS
Wilmington, Ohio

ISBN 978-1933197-647

Additional copies of *The Golden Lamb, Tales from the Innside* may be ordered directly from:

Orange Frazer Press
P.O. Box 214
Wilmington, OH 45177

Telephone 1.800.852.9332 for price and shipping information.
Website: www.orangefrazer.com

Library of Congress Cataloging-in-Publication Data

Compton, Fred, 1950-
  the Golden Lamb : tales from the innside / by Fred Compton.
    p. cm.
  ISBN 978-1-933197-64-7 (alk. paper)
  1. Golden Lamb (Lebanon (Warren County, Ohio)) 2. Lebanon (Warren County, Ohio)--History--Anecdotes. I. Title.
  F499.L4C66 2009
  977.1'763--dc22
                                    2009004849

THE GOLDEN LAMB

A. Blyth
December 2009
1st Edition

table of contents

introduction
200 years in the making

If there is one feeling I consistently came across in thirty-five years at the Golden Lamb in Lebanon, Ohio, it is that the hotel is a special place to those who visit. Whether it's once a week or once a year, guests regard the Golden Lamb as their restaurant, a family tradition that has been nurtured for generations.

During my tenure at "Ohio's Oldest Inn," I served three generations of guests. Young couples I first met in the 1970s had children who grew up, got married, and had children of their own, and then those children had their first dining experiences at the Golden Lamb.

Thousands of them polished their manners by sitting in one of the constantly repainted "booster seats" we kept in the coatroom. Their first experience with salad forks, meals in courses, and choosing their own desserts came under the watchful eye of a Golden Lamb server.

Pickled watermelon, corn relish, celery seed dressing, Swiss steak, and Shaker sugar pie are still on the menu. Jello salads still make their appearances on big holidays. The Golden Lamb still doesn't serve a public breakfast during the week (although it served almost 2,000 people on Mother's Day and Easter), still doesn't have an elevator, and, yes, if you call—even at three o'clock in the morning—a real person will answer the phone.

Dated and old fashioned?

Absolutely.

Food and customs from fifty years ago?

Yes, sir.

Will it ever change?

I hope not.

Things don't change much at the Golden Lamb and that's intentional. The guests want it that way. Guests want to walk in the door and see the same pictures on the wall, the same furniture in the lobby, and the same food on the menu. For the many guests, the hotel is a home away from home, and home doesn't change unless you want it to. "Ohio's Oldest Inn" is often described as traditional, conservative, and—to some people—downright stuffy.

They wouldn't have it any other way.

Conservative?

The Golden Lamb room reservation card still says, Guests Without Luggage Please Pay In Advance.

Tradition fosters security. And while lack of change is often looked upon with derision, it's a daily goal at the Golden Lamb. If the comments I heard for over thirty years are any indication, Golden Lamb guests long for that security and tradition.

I keep referring to the Golden Lamb as "the hotel." In one of my interviews with innkeeper Robert Jones in the 1970s, he said he was most proud that the Golden Lamb was one of the last surviving county seat hotels. For decades the Golden Lamb has been a source of pride for local residents, most of whom—at one time or another—celebrated special occasions at "the hotel."

Referring to the Golden Lamb as a "country inn" started in the early 1970s, but somehow it never took with me. When I started in 1966 it was "the hotel" and many like me refuse to change. So if you run into someone in Lebanon and they mention "the hotel," you know you're talking to somebody who has been around for a while. And if you should stumble across someone who refers to the Golden Lamb as "the ho-tel" (accent on the first syllable), listen to all that they have to say because they've been around long enough to see it all.

Filmmaker Ken Burns once wrote, "People forget that history contains the word story." Think of this book as a small encyclopedia, with lots of information on various topics in no particular order. There are stories on furniture, famous guests, food, architecture, holidays, artwork, and the Shakers. There are lots of stories about the things we did right and the things we did wrong.

The stories were told to me by hundreds of people, and although I took them at face value, with few chances of corroboration, they are all true, as far as I can tell.

This book will contain lots of current history, and if that phrase seems to be a contradiction in terms, it isn't. People assume that history is something that happened 200 years ago and then we read about it in a book. Nothing could be further from the truth.

Who would have thought a young Ronald Reagan, when he visited the Golden Lamb in 1968, would—just thirteen years later—become our eleventh presidential guest? In July of 1969 when I snuck up to the Grant Room and watched Neil Armstrong set foot on the moon, little did I know that he would become a neighbor and frequent guest of "Ohio's Oldest Inn."

So the history goes on. The 200 years contained here are just a small part. It is impossible to write down all I've learned about the hotel in over thirty years. Returning guests, an old piece of advertising, an older menu, all of it brings back a memory, many times a story.

For years, my good friend Carol Turner told me, "You've got to write it all down." It being the history of the hotel, and the stories I heard, researched, and experienced there. After all, during my tenure, I saw seven different presidents, six different governors, two major wars, and one Queen of England.

What follows is an unusual history book because it is not chronological. It will not start in 1803 and, I hope, will never end. Perhaps on the 250th anniversary of the hotel someone will write it all down again and add a few more chapters.

So it consists of facts and stories gathered by working the same street corner for over three decades and listening sincerely to anyone who had a story to tell about the hotel. And on these pages, the reader will also find the major topics that guests of the hotel ask about the most.

Many of the storytellers have long since passed away and won't be upset if I don't give them literary credit, and they won't be looking for royalties if I do.

Stories have a funny way of growing and expanding with each repetition. Memories grow fuzzy, dates are clouded, and the tales sometimes wind up being far superior to what really happened.

That will probably happen here.

A lot.

For those readers who are new to the Golden Lamb, or for those of you who were here as children and are now bringing your own children back, I hope you enjoy the history lesson.

And most of all, Carol, for you, here "it" is.

To Bob and Ginny Jones who started the whole thing . . .
To Joan Jones Portman who kept it going throughout the years . . .
To Jack Reynolds who always saw the possibilities . . .
This book is gratefully dedicated

THE GOLDEN LAMB

charles dickens and the golden lamb,
or, I don't care what you say about me, just spell my name right

Okay ... let's get him out of the way first.

Charles Dickens is the only Golden Lamb guest who gets his or her own chapter. Despite all their accomplishments and accolades, such distinguished guests as John Quincy Adams, Martin Van Buren, Mark Twain, Daniel Webster, and all the eleven dead presidents will be lumped together in a single chapter, but not Charles Dickens.

Certainly, Ronald Reagan and George W. Bush are the only modern-day presidents to visit "Ohio's Oldest Inn," and frequent guest Neil Armstrong was the first human being to walk on another celestial body. But despite their accomplishments, no single person has gotten the hotel more press and exposure than Charles Dickens did with his brief visit in April of 1842.

The newspaper coverage started two days after his visit and continues to this day. There have been more questions asked, more articles written, and more interest shown in Charles Dickens than any

3

of the inn's other political or literary heavyweights.

Charles Dickens is the only guest of the Golden Lamb to have both a bedroom and a dining room. Mark Twain has a bedroom but no dining room. Henry Clay has a dining room but no bedroom. Daniel Webster doesn't have either one and I still don't know why.

Dickens has both.

The irony of this situation is that Charles Dickens hated the Golden Lamb. He wrote terrible things about the inn in his book *American Notes,* which was published shortly after his visit. Dickens probably gave the Golden Lamb its first bad review in print. But I'm getting ahead of myself. Let's start at the beginning.

When the famed English author planned his grand tour of America in the winter and spring of 1842, it was with a three-fold purpose. He was gathering material for a book on the United States, which he would write upon his return to London. Travelogues were all the rage in Europe but nobody had written one about the United States. Dickens decided to be the first. Because interest in all things American was high throughout Europe, Dickens knew the book would be a best seller. The book did sell well, but it was savaged by critics on both sides of the Atlantic.

Dickens had a very naïve opinion of life in the United States. From across the Atlantic, he viewed America as somewhat utopian. Here was a country that was a republic, a country that had fought a war to become free and independent. There was no monarchy, no royalty, and no class distinction. Everyone had an equal voice in the government and officials were selected by a vote of the populace instead of being granted their positions by birth.

Unfortunately, when Dickens hopped off the steamship *Britannia* on January 22, 1842, any ideas of an American utopia were quickly washed away. In 1842 Dickens witnessed the beginnings of the American industrial revolution. Dickens had already lived through the European industrial revolution, having spent some of his childhood pasting labels on shoe polish bottles in a windowless London factory. So Dickens knew firsthand all the abuses—child labor, sweatshops— that came with rampant manufacturing. Not only had Dickens lived through it, he had written a couple of novels on the subject.

During an abbreviated trip through the South, Charles Dickens saw slavery for the first time. A slave auction on the docks of Charleston so sickened the author that he refused to travel farther and immediately returned north. The ideas of this republic of his imagination were dashed at every turn.

Dickens's second reason for touring the United States was much more basic. He needed cash. Worldwide fame and prolific literary output didn't make him particularly wealthy. Charles Dickens was saddled supporting a wife, and a large family in one of the most expensive cities on earth at the time—London.

Long before the days of movie rights, merchandising and product placement, Dickens only made money when he wrote. And even he could only write so many books in the course of a year. The famous English author was cash poor and needed a big score.

The money was to come via a series of lectures or "balls" in major cities where Dickens, for a price, would give readings of his works and discuss their inspiration. A frustrated actor, Dickens loved being on stage. The lectures would therefore serve a dual purpose, feeding both the author's pocket and his ego.

Dickens's third reason for visiting the United States was political and again revolved around money. Despite his proclivity towards charity and his lifelong struggle to improve the plight of the masses, money was never far from his mind. The idea of debtor's prisons, which still flourished in England, was a constant concern.

Throughout most of the author's life there was no universally accepted copyright law. Charles Dickens arrived in New York to find store after store crammed with pirated editions of his works for which he was being paid a penny.

And there wasn't one thing he could do about it.

The process of literary piracy in the nineteenth century was fairly straightforward. An unscrupulous American publisher would buy a copy of Dickens's latest book in London, bring it back to the United States, reset the book in type, print it, sell it, and keep all the profit.

American Notes, the book Dickens was researching, would be published in June of 1842, upon his return to London. It was reported that bootleg copies appeared in London in July of that year and were on the streets of New York in September.

Dickens's crusade was to buttonhole anyone who would listen, pleading for worldwide copyright protection for European authors. Dickens often cited the example of Sir Walter Scott, the famous English author who died destitute because his works were published worldwide without Scott receiving a penny.

In spite of his fame and persuasiveness, Charles Dickens's plea for literary protection fell on deaf ears. Totally unaware of the intricacies of copyright law and the political machinations needed to pass legislation in the United States, Dickens should have saved his breath for the stage. American legislators realized that the only American who would benefit from such protection would be Washington Irving, the New York author known for *The Legend of Sleepy Hollow* and *The Knickerbocker Tales*. Dickens, in fact, met Irving during his first lecture tour and received a reception that was described as "cordial but cool."

But perhaps the most compelling reason for the legislators'

lukewarm response was the economic state of the country in 1842. The United States was in the midst of a monetary depression and no self-respecting congressman looking at re-election was going to introduce legislation that would send money out of the country.

Dickens had no idea of his popularity when he visited in 1842. The English author was received with all the acclaim of a modern day rock star. When the *Britannia* docked in New York, thousands of people lined the docks shouting, "What happened to little Nell…what happened to little Nell?", referring to his novel *The Old Curiosity Shop*, the latest installment of which had yet to reach the United States.

Dickens was mobbed by well-wishers, glad-handers, and would-be hangers-on who wanted to be associated with the famous English author, and the author found Americans to be ill-mannered and extremely forward.

One of the customs Dickens couldn't understand was the American penchant for shaking hands, which he referred to as "pumping." The popular habit of American males spitting tobacco juice also filled the author with revulsion.

But it was the crowds that bothered him the most. Wherever Dickens traveled in the United States, he was surrounded by strangers.

And he hated it.

In *American Notes* Dickens describes his trip through northern

Ohio and says that even though his coach was small, drafty, and full of mail sacks ". . . we were blessedly alone."

Needless to say, Dickens was not in the best frame of mind when his party set out on April 22, 1842, from Cincinnati on a public coach headed north on what is now State Route 42. He did have a few kind words about the Queen City, calling it "the second most beautiful city I have seen in this country."

We lost out to Boston.

Dickens and party were traveling north through Ohio en route to Canada to view Niagara Falls. It is ironic that Charles Dickens loved to travel but hated to be away from England. Much like the early Spanish sailors who never traveled out of sight of land, Dickens became uneasy whenever he was away from England for more than a few weeks.

The solution was simple: Travel north through Ohio, then to New York and eventually to Canada. Ontario wasn't exactly London but it was under British control and Dickens could feel somewhat more at home. He was also fascinated by natural wonders in the United States. He had travelled as far west as St. Louis to view the Looking Glass Prairie and was now eager to see Niagara Falls.

He arrived in Lebanon on April 22, 1842, late in the afternoon, unannounced, and riding in a public coach. It was a cold April day and the young Dickens was dressed in a beaver hat and a heavy topcoat.

After alighting from the coach, Dickens and his party proceeded into what was then called the Bradley House, now known as the Golden Lamb. (There's a painting somewhere in the Golden Lamb titled *Charles Dickens Arriving At the Golden Lamb*. If you see it, just remember that in 1842 Dickens didn't look like that, the hotel didn't look like that, and there wasn't anybody around to greet him. So much for historical accuracy.)

The hotel was so named by then-innkeeper Calvin Bradley who had leased it from the Stubbs family, who had purchased it a year earlier. In naming the inn after himself, Calvin Bradley was following in the footsteps of numerous innkeepers before him. All had incorporated their own names into the title of the hotel.

Newspaper advertisements a decade earlier had trumpeted, "Mrs. Shares Hotel at The Sign of the Golden Lamb." Other references can be found to "Henry Shares Hotel At The Sign Of the Golden Lamb" or "The Stubbs House At The Sign Of the Golden Lamb." So Calvin Bradley wasn't feeding his own ego when he named the place after himself. He was just following tradition.

Dickens, after signing in as *C. Dickens London*, proceeded to sit at a public table with hotel residents and partake of a late afternoon meal. Few, if any, of the locals awaiting their dinner knew who Dickens was and cared even less.

And then it happened.

Charles Dickens made a simple request that shocked innkeeper Bradley. But perhaps it can best be described in Dickens's own words, taken from *American Notes*:

We dine soon after with boarders in the house and have nothing to drink but tea or coffee. As they are bad and the water worse, I ask for brandy. But it is a temperance hotel and spirits are not to be had for love nor money.

This preposterous forcing of unpleasant drink down the throats of reluctant travellers is not uncommon in America, but I never discovered that the scruples of such wincing landlords induced them to preserve any unusually nice balance between the quality of their fare and their scale of charges; on the contrary, I rather suspect them of diminishing one and exalting the other by way of recompense for the loss of their profit on the sale of spirituous liquors. After all, perhaps, the plainest course for persons of such tender conscience would be a total abstinence from tavern keeping.

Now for those of you not into nineteenth century Victorian syntax, Charles Dickens has just accused innkeeper Bradley of jacking up his prices to compensate for the fact that he didn't sell liquor. But he did it in such a civil, Dickensian way, it almost sounds like a compliment.

Dickens left the hotel in a huff and hopped on a coach that was conveniently waiting outside. His party headed north again on Route 42 and spent the night at the Xenia Hotel in Xenia, Ohio, which is now a short thirty-five-minute drive up the same road. The grand old hotel was heavily damaged during a tornado in 1974 and subsequently razed.

Charles Dickens

The preceding paragraph, for those who didn't catch it, let the cat out of the bag. No, Charles Dickens was *not* an overnight guest at the Golden Lamb like some of the other famous personages whose names adorn the hotel room doors. But he *was* a guest, even if they couldn't call him a completely satisfied customer. And that's good enough for the Golden Lamb and the hundreds of people who book months in advance to stay in the bedroom named in his honor.

Look at it this way. Even though Dickens gave the Golden Lamb its first bad review, he's made up for it with 167 years of good public relations. The fact that Dickens stormed out in a huff and then proceeded to blast the hotel on not one but two different continents served to put the place on the map for a lot of people.

And the Golden Lamb thanks him for it everyday.

that slab has held many a stiff, and other furniture-related stories

I'm going to cheat a little.

To be honest, I'm going to cheat a lot. The furniture stories in this chapter and others throughout the book appeared in print about twenty years ago in a wonderful publication called *Antique Review*. The tabloid style newspaper used to be called *Ohio Antique Review* until publisher Chuck Muller made it so popular he started sending it all over the United States and they had to change the name.

For years, the Golden Lamb published a supplement to the monthly publication but only in the month of January. In January—with snow on the ground and everybody broke from Christmas—the Golden Lamb needed the publicity and Chuck needed the advertisers. It was a match made in heaven, and we milked it for all it was worth.

See, I told you I was going to be honest.

We mailed newspapers, we gave them away, and we sent supplies to the other restaurants in our group to give away. We got around

9,000 on the third of January and I wanted them gone by the end of the month.

I supplied the editorial material and Chuck and his staff sold the ads. The copy was due by the middle of November, long before the Christmas rush started, with publication and delivery shortly after the first of the year.

In December of 1983, Chuck called me in a panic.

"I've got a hole to fill in the January edition," he said. "Send me a thousand words on ANYTHING...just make it quick!"

December is not the time to ask anyone at the Golden Lamb for anything extra. We were all so immersed in the holiday season, grinding it out day after day until January 2, that none of us had time for extra projects.

I quickly looked around and came up with an article of a little more than a thousand words, which seemed to pique the curiosity of regular readers, and a format that was repeated in subsequent issues for the next seven years.

"That Slab Has Held Many a Stiff" began a series of articles about overlooked pieces of furniture at "Ohio's Oldest Inn." The first year I wrote about the slab table in the lobby and the English coachman's bench beside it, two of my favorite pieces.

The effect was amazing. Just after the papers were made available in January of 1984, I began seeing guests walking the inn from ground floor to top floor, newspapers in hand, searching for the pieces I had written about, pieces they had been walking past for decades. We didn't include photographs in the article, so readers were on their own, identifying everything only by description and location.

Similar installments included "The Quilt That Wouldn't Die" and "Our Killer Bed." It was great fun to make guests and casual readers aware of the unique pieces that for the most part went unnoticed. I hoped that the articles made guests at the Golden Lamb aware that not all of the hotel's treasures are priceless pieces of Shaker.

For the sake of order, we'll start at the bottom and work our way to the fourth floor. That way, if you take this book and want to do your own exploring, there's only one trip up the stairs.

Because we're starting at the bottom, let's get one piece out of the way first. In the lobby, directly across from the front desk, sits what has to be everyone's favorite antique at the Golden Lamb. It is the one piece whose story I told a thousand times over the course of thirty-five years. It is the unique piece that drew *oohs* and *ahhs* day after day, decade after decade, the one piece that everyone wished to stick in the car trunk and take home.

I never liked it myself.

The Regina music box was a focal point of the Golden Lamb the entire time I worked there. That little square box with its seventy-odd disks entertained and amazed guests both young and old. The box played Christmas music in December, *Auld Lang Syne* on New Year's Eve, *My Old Kentucky Home* on Derby Day, the bridal chorus from *Lohengrin* when blushing brides came down the stairs, and patriotic melodies throughout July.

The Wurlitzer Company of Cincinnati assembled our box with works supplied by Regina. It originally shipped to a long-forgotten Vine Street retail store in Cincinnati called Taylor's. All my information comes from The Music Box Society of America, which diligently keeps track of such things for those who are interested.

Don't count me among them.

Regina supplied the music box works to various manufacturers who then installed them in boxes, or clocks, or even sideboards. The type of box we have came in three different sizes, with ours apparently being the most popular size because it pops up at antique shows from time to time. A smaller version took a disk the size of a $33^1/_3$ record album. (For readers under the age of 30, ask your parents to explain $33^1/_3$ record albums. They were very popular back in the olden years, such as 1972.)

A larger model was produced in which numerous disks were loaded vertically. It was the forerunner of a modern day jukebox, with coin-operated boxes and disks that could be selected and changed automatically.

The works of any Regina music box are fairly simple. If you could take it apart, the entire music mechanism could be held in the palm of your hand. The large wooden box is merely resonating space, which produces its great tone and volume.

On the front of each disk are groupings of holes, extending from the center to the outside. The holes are sometimes in clusters or in single lines. These are the "notes." On the backside of the disk are small protrusions, or "fingers," which correspond to the holes on the front. As the fingers strike the comb of the music box, notes are heard. Holes closest to the outside play

Regina music box

high notes. Those closest to the center play low notes. The more holes clustered together, the more notes that are played.

The music box at the Golden Lamb is in near perfect condition with one exception: once wound up, you can't turn the thing off. The on-off lever refuses to function and the mainspring on the inside that drives the motor has to wind down completely before the music stops.

I can't tell you how many times I've been forced to listen to *Jingle Bells* or *The Handicap March* over and over again long after a well-meaning guest who just had to hear the music box walked away after listening for about forty-five seconds.

The music box now sitting in the lobby is not the same one that was there when I first came to work in 1966. That particular Regina was on loan from a friend of the owners, Robert and Virginia Jones. When the management of the inn changed hands in 1969, the friend came and got his music box. Manager Jack Reynolds thought it was no big deal. What was one less piece of furniture in a place filled to the rafters with valuable antiques? Nobody would miss it.

Wrong.

Almost immediately the questions started: *What happened to the music box? Did you sell the music box? Was the music box stolen?* We were regaled with music box memories on a daily basis, as well as comments about how the hotel just wasn't the same without it.

Jack began a search for a "new" old music box to replace the Regina, which had been such a focal point. A few months later, a suitable replacement was found in northern Kentucky, with a stand and an excellent collection of disks. Once again, things were back to normal at "Ohio's Oldest Inn."

Across the lobby from the music box, close to the fireplace, is one of the most overlooked pieces in the hotel. Sitting over there is a long low table with a noticeable depression in the middle. Most people dismiss it, preferring to listen to the music box or stare weepy-eyed at some piece of Shaker. But that little nondescript table has a fascinating history—and a somewhat grisly function.

Guests who did notice it assumed that it graced the dining room or parlor of some long forgotten family, but nothing could be further from the truth. This particular table provided no service to the living but great service to the dead.

Properly called a "cooling table," this sturdy piece of furniture was rescued from a Warren County mortuary. Knowing its previous owners, readers can only imagine what was "cooled" on the table. The depression in the middle was for…well, let's just say physics tells us that liquids always flow to their lowest point.

Close to the cooling table is what I believe to be the single oldest antique within the Golden Lamb. Ironically, this piece is not American but English. The gray, square-bottomed bench with the sagging bottom and the 200-year-old paint is a "coachman's bench," pedigreed to the year 1792. Over the years, that particular bench supported hundreds of thousands of travelers waiting to hear those magic words: "Table is ready for the Smith party of four please…Smith party of four."

On the vertical front of the bench are two small knobs, one on either end. Not for decoration, these knobs served as legs when the top was folded out. Inside the hollow bench are pegs, used to support a hammock. Due to his social standing, a coachman would not have been due a room of his own at a respectable English inn. This antique hide-a-bed ultimately became his resting-place for the night. Though I never personally attempted to recreate the bench's original use, I can

Coachman's bench

only assume the sleeping conditions were somewhat claustrophobic.

The bench, being hollow, also makes a great sound when unattended kids swing their feet against the front panel. On these occasions I would politely approach the parents and say, "Sir (or madam), would you please indicate to your son (or daughter) that it is not proper behavior to BANG THEIR LEGS AGAINST OUR IRREPLACEABLE 200-YEAR-OLD ENGLISH COACHMAN'S BENCH. Thank you."

Before we leave the lobby, let's talk briefly about the two pistols mounted over the mantle. I don't know how old they are, how much they are worth, or even where they came from originally. But how they came to rest under the sign of the Golden Lamb is a great story.

The time was just before World War II. Two English engineers working in Dayton at Wright Field (later to become Wright-Patterson Air Force Base), were lodging at the Golden Lamb, then owned by innkeeper Robert Jones. Jones struck up a particular friendship with these guests, due both to the length of their stay and the fact that they were as fascinated with American history as he was.

The two pistols belonged to one of the engineers, perhaps being a keepsake passed down through the generations. Because the engineer knew he would be away from home for some time, the pistols traveled with him for safekeeping.

All was well until troubling reports began filtering in from Europe. As Germany expanded militaristically and England geared up for war, it was simply a matter of time until the two would be summoned to put their talents to use on the home front.

When the inevitable summons arrived, the pair began packing for the return trip to England. But the owner of the pistols felt unsure of what to do with his precious possession. Neither man knew what was waiting for them or how long they would be gone.

The decision was made to leave the firearms in the capable hands of innkeeper Jones. He bid a fond farewell to his guests, vowing to see them when the war was over. The pistols were placed in Jones's own home until the return of their rightful owner.

Once the war was over, Jones awaited some word from the British engineers. After a suitable period of time, the pistols were put on display at the hotel. Over sixty-five years later the two pistols, so precious to the owner that he deposited them a half a world away, are still being held for safekeeping under the sign of the Golden Lamb, awaiting their rightful owner.

There are a couple of other items to glance at before we leave the lobby. Next to the mantle is a large plantation desk, which holds the guest register. I'd love to have a nickel for every person who began their career at the Golden Lamb by filling out an application at that desk. The only thing I know about the desk is that it is NOT SHAKER. People look at the simple design and the clean lines and automatically assume Brother So-and-So crafted it.

He didn't.

On the right side of the doorway to the Lebanon (Dining) Room is a piece that has entertained both children and adults for decades. A print entitled *The Great Battleship Maine in Havana Harbor Before and After the Explosion* sits on a small table next to the candy and is an object that I call our antique video game.

The print, housed in a wooden box, is lit from the rear by pressing a button. Without the backlight all you see is a colorful portrait of *The Maine* in Havana Harbor. But push the button and another image appears, one of an exploding ship complete with underwater bomb, a Spanish fort on the coast, and—for emphasis—a few bodies flying through the air. Undoubtedly, this pre-twentieth century piece was used to incite patriotic spirit in the country and drum up support for the Spanish-American War.

Innkeeper Jackson Reynolds found this piece in the middle 1970s in the form of a print. Undoubtedly, in its original form, it was held up to a light in order to see the image on the reverse side. It was Jack's ingenious idea to build the box with light bulbs on the inside to make viewing easier.

The antique video game is now entertaining its second generation of guests at the Golden Lamb. Young and old alike still press the button and blow up a piece of American history. It continues to amaze me that video-drenched kids are still fascinated by a light bulb . . . behind a picture.

Walking straight ahead from *The Battleship Maine* takes you into the Lebanon Room, which for historical purposes is the oldest room in the place. This was the site of Jonas Seaman's original log tavern, built in 1803. For some reason, totally unknown to me, the Lebanon Room wasn't all that popular with guests. I can think of only two sets of guests who wanted to sit there and nowhere else.

Maybe it was the fact that people passed through the room on their

Shaker chest

way to the gift shop. Maybe it was because people passed through that room on their way out of the bar. Maybe it was the wallpaper. I don't know. But for some reason it was always tough to get people to sit in that room.

I always liked the room myself.

Throughout the years whenever someone came in and asked to be seated in the "old" part of the hotel, I immediately started for the Lebanon Room. "Oh, no," they would say. "We want to sit over there," indicating the north dining rooms, "in the old section."

I always knew where they wanted to sit, but it was a good excuse to give them a quick history lesson on Golden Lamb architecture. Unfortunately, I never converted anyone and always wound up taking them to the "old" section, which wasn't as old as where I wanted to put them in the first place.

If you do walk into the true "old" section of the building, look immediately to your left. Sitting there is supposedly the best piece of

Shaker furniture in the hotel. To anyone coming to our place looking for Shaker artifacts, this solid cherry "doors over drawers" chest is regarded as the Holy Grail.

Shaker aficionados run their hands over the surface, marveling at the workmanship and detail. The patina of the wood seems to glow. The sides are made of solid cherry planks of a size I'm told is unavailable today. This one-of-a-kind chest should probably be in a museum to be studied by scholars and furniture craftsmen.

We used it to store menus.

Therein lies one of the great aspects of the Golden Lamb. The furniture isn't roped off or behind a glass case for study at a distance of ten feet. They use it . . . EVERYDAY. Visitors are allowed, even encouraged to touch the furniture and even sleep on it. (Or is it sleep in it?) The hotel was a hands-on museum before anyone ever came up with the term.

But back to the chest.

For years, I asked the same question to all those Shaker geeks who stood misty-eyed in front of our menu chest: "What makes this piece so great?"

The answer was always the same: "It just is."

This particular chest had a specific function, which has yet to be discovered. One of the basic traits of most Shaker furniture is that—all being handmade—no two pieces were exactly alike. Each piece had a specific purpose. Shaker expert Chuck Muller once told me that this chest might have been made for a particular person. The doors-over-drawers design is unique. The pigeonholes on the inside of the upper section were there for a specific purpose. Perhaps they held papers, documents, folded napkins, or recipes. The possibilities are endless.

But what makes the chest at the Golden Lamb truly intriguing are the two secret drawers hidden within its doors section. There are four horizontal drawers visible between the upper doors and the lower large drawers. The two drawers on the outside, when pulled out, are the same depth as the chest. The two center drawers, when pulled out, are only half size. Behind those two short drawers are two "secret drawers" that wouldn't be noticed unless you knew where to look. For years, even I didn't know they were there.

Remember all those weepy-eyed Shaker enthusiasts whom I asked, "What makes this piece so great?" My second question always was, "By the way, what did the Shakers have to hide from people?" What did a religion based on openness, honesty, and simplicity, a religion that welcomed examination, have to hide?

Just like the true function of the chest, we'll probably never know.

The Lebanon Room also houses a set of portraits and the interest lies not in who they are but in what they are. Sound confusing? Read on.

On the north wall are portraits of a very stern-looking gentleman and an equally grim-looking female. The gentleman is some long forgotten nineteenth century postmaster of the city of Cincinnati and the lady, of course, is his wife.

These "paired portraits" are one of two sets at the Golden Lamb. Both sets date from the nineteenth century and despite their appearances, they were relatively inexpensive in origin. Limners, itinerant artists who traveled the countryside, set up shop in small towns and painted these types of portraits.

The portraits were inexpensive because when the artist came to town the portraits were already done, except for the head. A husband and wife could sit down, have their faces painted on a body that was probably painted months earlier. In this way, it was very quick and inexpensive to have a portrait to hang on the wall. In some instances, the hands would be painted on the female portrait, in case the lady had family jewelry she wanted to show off.

For the most part, these paintings were always of a husband and wife, hence the name "paired portraits." In some instances, though, children were evident. The Warren County History Center has a set of paired portraits of siblings hanging in Glendower Museum on Cincinnati Avenue in Lebanon.

If you look very closely at the paintings in the Lebanon Room you will see how cracked the finish is. These paintings, in order to keep the cost down, were done on heavy paper instead of canvas. The other set, which are somewhat larger, resides in the Presidents' Dining Room on the second floor.

There's not really anything else of major interest in this room. The corridor on the south side, which leads back to the Black Horse Tavern, contains a pair of nineteenth century gaming tables that are unique only from the fact that tables like this aren't made anymore.

Take a look at the tops of the tables and notice how they are hinged at the back. The tops are, indeed, double in size of what is normally seen. The tops fold out and swivel on the base, making a four-sided surface for cards or board games while the base provides built-in storage. They're clever little tables but hardly worth mentioning.

Does that last statement surprise you? If so, perhaps this is as good a time as any to lay out my opinions about antiques and collecting.

I don't like antiques, never have.

If this sounds strange coming from a person who lived and worked in an historic property for almost thirty-five years, I'm sorry.

No, I'm not.

I recognize and respect the value, both monetary and historic, of the furniture at the Golden Lamb. I appreciate the importance, the workmanship, the individuality, and the craftsmanship that have gone into each and every piece. I appreciate it, I respect it, and I recognize it, but I don't want to live with it. My own house is so modern, I don't have a magazine that's a month old. This mania of searching week after week, month after month, and shop after shop to find "just the right piece" for "just the right place" is an obsession I'll never understand. This passion of prowling antique shops and shows to find the top of a Staffordshire sugar bowl so a collection can be complete is a mystery to me.

Some readers might be saying, "Where would the Golden Lamb be if Robert and Virginia Jones hadn't started collecting all that furniture over seventy years ago?"

Well, the Joneses didn't start out as antique collectors.

But that's another chapter.

Photo of Golden Lamb, early 1900s

a few words about Henry Clay, Harriet Beecher Stowe, and all those dead presidents

The Golden Lamb has made a fortune off one English author and twelve presidents.

What's ironic is that the author was a cranky Englishman who left to seek accommodations on up the road rather than spend the night in a "temperance hotel," and ten of the twelve U.S. presidents were arguably the worst chief executives this country had the misfortune to endure.

With the exception of John Quincy Adams and Ronald Reagan, none of them would ever make anyone's top ten list of presidential administrations. But they were here, they were or went on to be president, and that's good enough for the Golden Lamb. But once again I'm getting ahead of myself. Let's start at the beginning.

For the uninitiated, over the past 200 years the Golden Lamb has had the honor of hosting a who's who of literary and political figures in the United States. Bellying up to the bar over the past two centuries have been the likes of Henry Clay, Mark Twain, Daniel Webster, Harriet

Beecher Stowe, and twelve . . . count 'em, twelve United States presidents.

And for perhaps the one millionth time, YES, ANYONE WHOSE NAME IS ON A DOOR WAS A GUEST AT THE GOLDEN LAMB AT ONE TIME OR ANOTHER. You would be astounded how many times in the course of my career someone asked, "Was Charles Dickens really a guest here?" Or, "Does Henry Clay's name on the door mean he actually stayed here?"

Did people think they just picked those names out of a hat? If they had, don't you think they would have picked better names than Marcus Mote (Room 1) or Edwin Forrester (Room 18)?

Author's Note: Marcus Mote and Edwin Forrester were both wonderful individuals with great accomplishments during their lifetimes. They probably also have a lot of living relatives who might take offense at the preceding paragraph.

Yes, they were *all* here, sometimes more than once. Some of the reasons are downright interesting. Some are pretty boring, but they all deserve to be told.

The reason most of those great Americans wound up in Lebanon, Ohio, and at the Golden Lamb was geographic. During most of the nineteenth century, Lebanon was exactly one day's ride from Cincinnati. If you hopped on a stage at eight in the morning, then eight hours later when you were tired, the horses were tired, and it was dark and not safe to travel, Lebanon is where you were. And there was the three-story brick Federal style hotel at the corner of Main and Broadway, where it had been since as early as 1844.

After I answered that question, the next one was always, "OK, smart guy . . . WHY were Charles Dickens, Henry Clay, and all those presidents travelling one day's ride from Cincinnati?"

The answer again involves geography, and Henry Clay is the prime example. Clay lived in Kentucky but worked in Washington, D.C. Lacking the convenience of a super highway, light rail, or the red-eye out of Lexington, when Clay wanted to go change the course of history he couldn't travel due east because of a little roadblock called the Allegheny Mountains.

Oh, yeah, and there was no road.

Clay traveled either by carriage or horseback north through Kentucky, crossed the river into Cincinnati and up what is now State Route 42, winding up—after a hard day's ride—in Lebanon. He then continued north on the road to Zanesville, Ohio, and picked up the National Road, which was the major east-west route across the mountains.

During the nineteenth century, Clay was a guest numerous times on his way back and forth to Washington, D.C. It is rumored that

Clay's young daughter Eliza died in our hotel in 1832 of what was described only as a "childhood illness." I say "rumored" because my long-time friend John Zimkus, Lebanon's premier historian, is sure that Eliza Clay died at the Indian Chief Hotel on Mulberry Street. John is much more of a historian than I am, so maybe he's right.

Many of our famous guests were travelling that south-to-north route to go west-to-east. Some were not. So with that in mind, let's get down to cases. Charles Dickens got his own chapter so we can skip him. We just covered Henry Clay, so let's move on to some of those dead presidents that we've all grown to know and love.

John Quincy Adams, the sixth president of the United States, visited Lebanon and stayed at the Golden Lamb in 1843, a year after Dickens's momentous visit. Adams was not president when he visited, having served as president from 1825-1829. He was in fact a congressman from Massachusetts when he was here, an office he held until his death in 1848.

Remember that long story I told about Henry Clay traveling south-to-north to go west-to-east?

Forget it.

John Quincy Adams was in fact traveling south into Cincinnati when he visited the hotel in 1843. Adams was to be the keynote speaker at the dedication of the Cincinnati Observatory, a powerful telescope built on Mount Ida in Cincinnati. Another guest of the Golden Lamb, Ormsby McKnight Mitchel, built the telescope. (He is listed in our first history book and on the door of his room as "Ormsby Mitchel.")

Henry Clay room

Cincinnati rolled out the red carpet for Adams to the point of renaming the landscape in his honor. Gone was Mount Ida, replaced by, of course . . . Mount Adams.

Harriet Beecher Stowe, "the little lady who started the great big war," wasn't particularly famous or radical when she came to Lebanon. Her famous novel, *Uncle Tom's Cabin,*was several decades away and Harriet was here trying to turn a buck.

Harriet and her sister Catherine came to Lebanon to establish a girls' finishing school. In 1832, the ladies took out ads in *The Western Star*, the local newspaper, stating they had "taken rooms at Mrs. Share's Hotel" to interview applicants for their proposed school.

The "Mrs. Share" mentioned in the ad was Mary Share, who had taken over the inn after the death of her husband, Henry Share.

Apparently, the market wasn't quite right for a girls school in Lebanon. Harriet and her sister failed to interview a single applicant. Both returned to Cincinnati and on to bigger and better things. At least Harriet did. What Catherine did I have no idea. They never named a room after her, so I never bothered to check.

Most of the presidents (who weren't really presidents when they were here) were passing through on one political mission or another. Just for the record, those presidents we exploited in our advertising are as follows: William Henry Harrison, Benjamin Harrison, Martin Van Buren, John Quincy Adams, Rutherford B. Hayes, William Howard Taft, James Garfield, William McKinley, Ulysses S. Grant, Warren G. Harding, Ronald Reagan, and George W. Bush.

Looking at our distinguished guests and their accomplishments, we see that William Henry Harrison's great distinction is the shortest presidential term on record. Giving his inauguration speech in 30-degree weather without a hat, or a coat, or an HMO, Harrison contracted pneumonia and died thirty days into his first and only term, not having done much of anything.

William Howard Taft didn't even want to be president and saw his administration as a stepping stone to the job he really wanted: sitting on the United States Supreme Court.

If you look up poor James Garfield in any history textbook, you will find the same sentence: shot by a disappointed office seeker.

Such is *his* legacy.

Ulysses S. Grant swept into office by his success during the Civil War and was the only president ever arrested while in office. He got a speeding ticket for driving a coach too fast up Pennsylvania Avenue. Good soldier that he was, Grant paid the ticket himself. He was also embroiled in the Credit Mobilier scandal while in office, a name you probably remember from a long-ago history class. During the scandal, the majority of Grant's administration was bought off to secure favorable rights-of-way for the new Union Pacific Railroad. Ironically, the Department of Justice was created during Grant's troubled tenure in the White House.

When he left the White House in 1877 he was, by all accounts, a wealthy man. Nobody took the time to tell him that ex-presidents are supposed to get richer once they're out of office. Grant promptly proceeded to lose millions in bad investments on Wall Street. Bankrupt and with throat cancer, it was only through the gracious help of another Golden Lamb guest—Mark Twain—that Grant managed to live out his days in relative comfort.

Twain gave Grant a generous advance on his memoirs and 75 percent of the book's royalties. Grant finished the memoirs just days before he died in July of 1885. And for those of you who are still wondering, he is buried in Grant's Tomb, which, by the way, is the largest mausoleum in North America.

My personal favorite among the Golden Lamb guests has to be Warren G. Harding. Harding, who never wanted to be anymore than mayor of Marion, Ohio, presided over one of the most scandal-ridden administrations in United States history. Harding filled his administration with political cronies and personal friends who knew nothing about running the government. His secretary of the interior, Albert B. Fall, was the first cabinet member in history to go to jail. His administration was responsible for the Teapot Dome Scandal, another name you heard in a history class long ago. Harding's old friend (and soon to be convict) Harry Fall gave private oil companies the rights to tap strategic oil reserves on government land. Perhaps "gave" is the wrong word. For valuable consideration, Secretary Fall allowed companies to drill.

Historians have documented at least two affairs that Harding had prior to being elected to office, one of which produced a child. Even after he was in office, rumors continued to consume Washington, D. C., concerning Harding's scandalous behavior.

Harding had several firsts in his administration. When he ran for president, women were allowed to vote for the first time. Given his matinee-idol looks and a strong speaking voice, he captured the hearts of the newly enfranchised female population. He was the first president to ride in his inaugural parade in an automobile. He was the first president to have his inaugural ceremony broadcast on the radio.

This was not a good thing.

After the ceremony concluded, a British reporter described Harding's inaugural address as being "the most illiterate statement ever uttered by the head of a civilized nation."

Perhaps Harding himself best summed up his administration when he said, "I am not fit for this job and shouldn't be here."

Lew Hudnall painting of lobby

yes, Virginia, there really was a Sister Lizzie
a very brief history of the Shakers

You can't throw a rock in Lebanon without hitting something that says Shaker. Despite the disappearance of the Protestant religious denomination over a century ago, this town (and that includes the Golden Lamb) still exploits the Shaker connection for all it's worth.

We started it, I guess. Golden Lamb owners Robert and Virginia Jones began collecting Shaker furniture and artifacts as early as 1940, long before a Shaker chest became more expensive than the average three-bedroom house. Robert Jones admired the furniture's lines and construction, and over four decades, he and his wife amassed one of the most envied Shaker collections in the country. Many of the pieces are on display at the Warren County History Center, just two doors south of the hotel. The Joneses donated so much of their collection to the center in 1974, the Golden Lamb spearheaded a campaign called

"History For The Future," resulting in the addition of another wing to the museum, appropriately named The Robert and Virginia Jones Shaker Gallery.

The Golden Lamb is full of Shaker stuff, from the basement to the top floor. I've seen guests stand and salivate in front of a particular piece, then trudge all the way to the fourth floor in the middle of July (when the heat is at its worst) just to stand and stare at the two Shaker display rooms. I lived with this furniture and these artifacts for over thirty years, and spent countless hours talking about the secret drawers in the big cherry chest, explaining the particular functions of the yarn swift hanging in the lobby or the mammoth cheese press in the Shaker (Dining) Room. So let me offer my opinion of Shaker furniture: I wouldn't give you a nickel for a whole houseful of these pieces, not if I had to live with them day after day. As I previously mentioned, I am not an antique-y kind of guy. If you want to pay six figures for a one-of-a-kind piece of Shaker furniture, go right ahead. I wish I was the person selling it to you. But don't expect me to get all weepy over some 100-year-old chest just because a celibate carpenter made it and it's got great dovetails in the drawers.

Okay, that's my confession. Now, let me give you enough pertinent information to bluff your way through a conversation on Shakers and their furniture.

The United Society of Believers in Christ's Second Appearing (later to be known as Shakers) originated in the eighteenth century in France with a fundamentalist society called the Camisards. In 1769, two Britons, James and Jane Wardley, began preaching the religion in England and added the new twist of twitching, strange movements and outcries they called "operations of the powers of God." One of the earliest converts was a woman named Ann Stanley, born February 29, 1736, in Manchester, England. Uneducated and unattractive, Stanley was particularly taken with the Wardleys, as they were with her. Soon after her religious conversion, she began to have visions. She foresaw the end of the world and Christ's re-appearance in female form. Jane Wardley swore this vision was spelled out in the Psalms. If you want to look for it, go ahead. Call me if you find it. I never did.

The fact that Ann Stanley had visions and trances was not unusual, given her educational level and perhaps a subconscious desire to please the Wardleys. Unfortunately, though, she had more than a few of her visions at high noon in the middle of a busy London street, and consequently was locked up. In 1770, she had another vision in which Christ appeared to her in her jail cell and they were married. The Christ-like female form Ann Stanley had predicted would return to earth was . . . guess who?

Though you might think I make light of this event, it was a major turning point in the Shaker religion. The major religions of the world are all different, but they have one thing in common. The central supreme figure is always depicted as a . . . male. But suddenly, here's Ann Stanley with a religion where the Supreme Being is now a female. Kind of puts a different spin on things, doesn't it? Needless to say, the Church of England didn't appreciate people roaming around the countryside proclaiming that not only was a divine being in their midst, but that divine being was a woman. Like Stanley, believers were persecuted and imprisoned on a regular basis.

In 1774, "Mother Ann Lee," as she was now called, had yet another vision. While in prison (yet again), she saw a land for her people with more tolerance, more freedom, and a chance for her to truly lead the church without fear of persecution. That land? You guessed it. America. Mother Ann and eight true believers (including her ex-husband) set sail for North America and on August 6, 1774, arrived in New York. The group marched from the docks, up Pearl Street, and stopped in front of a house owned by Abner Cunningham. As luck would have it, the owner was relaxing on his front porch at the time.

Mother Ann pointed at Mr. Cunningham, "called him by name," and proclaimed: "I am commissioned of the almighty God to preach the everlasting gospel in America and an angel has commanded me to come to this house and to make a home for my people." Not knowing what else to do, the bewildered Abner Cunningham said, "Works for me," or words to that effect.

Stanley and her followers stayed for almost two years before purchasing land north of Albany, New York, and establishing the first Shaker colony, which they named Watervliet.

So now you have a band of people with English accents trying to establish a foothold in America at the height of the American Revolution. They had a new religion, too. Most Americans didn't roll out the red carpet quite like Abner Cunningham. The United Society was first viewed as a group of English spies—infiltrators who came here to learn plans for the revolution and report back to England. When Americans learned that this stalwart group had no interest in politics, money, or the military, they probably decided that the United Society of Believers was just a little unusual.

The newly arrived Shakers presented some pretty radical behavior to those around them in their newfound home. Members were celibate (more on that later). They lived in communal societies outside of the central population, seeking to isolate themselves from the temptations of "the world outside." They grew their own food, made their own clothes, and made most of their own furniture and implements.

And perhaps the most radical idea of all, one that probably shook the foundations of eighteenth century America, the Shakers believed that women were equal. A woman could own property, sign documents, and handle money just like a man? Absolutely. Remember that the spiritual head of the church, Ann Stanley, was a woman. Therefore, women and men, in principle, had equal status within the United Society. For every Shaker elder, there was an eldress who had an equal voice in the day-to-day decision-making.

Let's not forget that they "danced in church," as un-initiated Americans viewed them. These "manifestations of God" (which were, in fact, pantomimes) were seen by outsiders as just another nail in the coffin of the Shakers.

So what drove these people to shun worldly possessions, cohabitation and money in order to slave away all day making perfect furniture? Why were their beliefs and lifestyle so plain and unadorned by most standards? Let's jump ahead to the twentieth century for a possible explanation.

In the early part of the century, artist and photographer Charles Sheeler took a keen interest in the Shakers. Sheeler described his particular style of painting and photography as "Precisionism" because he tended to photograph industrial and constructed objects such as factories and machinery. When he began photographing and painting Shaker furniture and buildings, he said, "I don't like these things because they are old, but in spite of it. . . . I'd like them still better if they were made yesterday, because then they would afford proof [that] the same kind of creative power is continuing."

In a 1928 essay about furniture (not only Shaker furniture but furniture in general), Sheeler said, "Ornamentation is often applied to conceal uncertainty." Think about that statement for a second. Suppose you were building a table and wanted to make it out of cherry wood. But cherry is an expensive wood, hard to find, and not the easiest wood to work. So you choose an easier and cheaper wood instead, like pine or oak, and then stain it to look like cherry. Or, maybe you want to lay a floor in your home, but the joints are not as tight as you would like them and perhaps there are a few knots and bad sections of grain in the wood. When the floor is done, it is serviceable but less than perfect. What can you do? Well, the floor can be stained or painted, or covered with a rug to hide the imperfections.

Indeed, "ornamentation is often applied to conceal uncertainty." But folks familiar with Shaker furniture and Shaker construction already know that very little of the group's furniture was stained, and the floors in their buildings and meeting halls were rarely painted or covered with rugs. Why? Because there was no "uncertainty" to hide. Every piece of furniture, whether used in the community or sold to the outside world, was a model of perfection. A Shaker carpenter would take just as much care with cupboard doors in an attic (which the average visitor would never see) as he would with the doors in a meeting hall that everyone would see every day. One of the basic precepts of the Shaker religion was to create a heaven on earth, and heaven was perfect.

The noted Shaker historian, Thomas Merton, perhaps expressed it best when he said, "The easiest way to understand the grace and precision of a Shaker chair is to realize that it was made by a person who firmly believed that an angel might one day come and sit on it." The Shakers' desire for perfection, their simple unadorned lifestyle, their willingness to open their homes and meetings to thorough inspection by the outside world, typified a lifestyle devoid of "ornamentation" and totally lacking in "uncertainty."

Though hard to imagine in this day and age, try to picture a typical Shaker community with no retail stores, no restaurants, no theaters, no taverns, no entertainment of any type. The Shakers had no police, no jail, little if any crime, no court systems, no poverty, no hunger, no unemployment, no homelessness, and no taxes. Everyone in the community, for as long as they cared to stay, had a roof over their heads, food on their table, clothes on their back and a job.

Despite their cloistered lifestyle, the Shakers were wonderfully inventive people who gave numerous time-saving and labor-saving devices to the outside world—and the emphasis here is on the word *gave*. Most of the simple innovations the Shakers devised were never patented or controlled.

If you have a pen in your pocket, thank the Shakers. They didn't invent the writing device, but they did perfect the metal pen. Do you have a washing machine at home? Thank the Shakers. Once again, the United Society of Believers didn't invent the washing machine, but by 1884 they were receiving numerous orders from hospitals, hotels, and restaurants for the "improved Shaker washing machine" that was being manufactured in eastern communities. If you have any permanent press fabric in that washing machine, once again thank the Shakers. In the mid-1800s, they developed a solution into which they could dip a garment, press it off with a hot iron, and have it remain wrinkle-free for several days.

The list goes on and on. The common clothespin, the circular saw, flat brooms, cut nails, and mail-order catalogues all sprang from the Shakers' inventive minds. And all were given freely to the outside world without any thought of profit.

Perhaps the most striking aspect of the Shaker religion was celibacy. Ann Stanley had been married early in her life and bore four children, all of whom died young. In England in the mid-1700s, the infant mortality rate was sky high. But Mother Ann, it is believed, took this as a sign from God that men and women should not procreate.

Married couples could enter the Shaker religion, but ceased being married when they did. If they had children, they were raised in another part of the community. The Shakers did not believe in the immediate family (i.e. mother, father, sister, brother, aunt, uncle, cousin, and so on). The entire community was the family. All members were your brothers and sisters. Mother Ann was your spiritual mother and Christ your spiritual father. The familiar Shaker Tree of Life shows all names attached to a single trunk. The branches are attached to, and flow from, a single source.

Living a celibate lifestyle made it impossible to make any new Shakers. The United Society relied on external conversion to increase their ranks and took in orphans to increase the membership in the community. The Shakers hit their peak about the time of the Civil War and then slowly dwindled in number. Union Village, the settlement near Lebanon, was founded in 1802 and became one of the larger communities, lasting until the early part of the twentieth century. Supposedly the last Shaker left in Lebanon, James Fennessey, became a schoolteacher and lived his final years at the Golden Lamb.

Now, about the furniture.

Shaker furniture has been admired and sought-after ever since they sold their first chair by mail order. The Shakers saw the advantages of in-home catalogues long before Sears had a clue as to the possibilities of marketing by mail. Over the years the furniture has gotten more expensive and harder to find. I was exaggerating, of course, when I previously said that a desirable Shaker chest today costs as much as an average three-bedroom home, but you get the point.

The Shaker collection at the Golden Lamb is scattered throughout five floors and for the most part is used every day. Purists have recoiled in horror when they see a hostess stuff napkins into the drawers of the big Shaker chest. Others have gone into screaming fits when they see our perhaps one-of-a-kind tailor's bench piled high with bread and butter plates.

Were any Shakers left in Lebanon today, however, I believe they would be proud of what the Golden Lamb is doing. The furniture was built to be used, not stared at in a museum setting. The hotel doesn't charge admission to see it. They don't discourage anyone from examining the furniture throughout the building, pulling out the drawers, taking measurements and photographs, and so on. I'm sure the United Society would have wanted it that way and would have wondered what all the fuss was about.

So as long as you promise not to chain yourself to a Shaker table to prevent its use in the twenty-first century, I'll give you a quick tour of the Golden Lamb's best and most unusual pieces. Just remember, if I make a few sarcastic remarks along the way, please forgive me. Like the

Shakers, I don't know what all the fuss is about.

Number one on the list is the previously discussed "doors over drawers" chest in the Lebanon Room. This piece seems to evoke some mystical power over any Shaker enthusiast who sees it.

Next up is the large tailor's bench on the north wall of the Shaker Room. It's the piece you see piled high with bread and butter plates every day and used as a service stand during dining hours. The bench is not nearly as attractive as the chest, but people who know, tell me it's one-of-a-kind.

In the Shaker Room are lots of little artifacts hanging from authentic Shaker pegs around the perimeter of the room. (These pegs were rescued from Union Village, where, in the middle to late 1950s, many of the Shaker buildings had fallen into disrepair and were routinely burned by the fire department, for practice. Fortunately, a lot of the interior millwork was recovered before it got torched.) The uses for most of these artifacts are pretty self-evident, although most people don't recognize a starch strainer or a seed stripper when they see one. If you've never seen a starch strainer or a seed stripper, have dinner at the Golden Lamb and just study them hanging on the wall. You'll figure it out.

I once interrupted a Shaker aficionado from the University of Cincinnati who was intently studying a breadboard in the Shaker Room. It looked like an old piece of wood to me, but the "expert" declared it the best Shaker piece we had. When I asked why, he took a deep breath and dramatically replied, "It speaks to me." I quickly left him alone, in case he wanted to continue his conversation in private or perhaps strike up a dialogue with the cheese press hanging on the rear wall. People get freaky around this stuff.

In the lobby, hanging above the steps to the Dickens Room, is a Shaker yarn swift. The swift was made by one of those celibate carpenters I mentioned earlier, but not just for use by the United Society. The Shakers made these things by the thousands and sold them to the public. If you want to know how this clever device works, stare at it long enough and, like I said, you'll figure it out.

The Lamb Shop on the hotel's lower level has some unique pieces of Shaker furniture, used to display everything from Christmas cards to candy. Pay particular attention to the low red wash chest if it's still there, regarded as a particularly valuable piece. If it's not there, well, it probably got moved. So sue me.

On the second floor, you will notice a very large Shaker seed chest on the landing beside the steps, along with a small collection of Shaker seed boxes and a small Shaker table. If you have the energy, take a walk up to the fourth floor and look at the two Shaker display rooms. Here are some of the finest examples of eastern and western Shaker you will ever see. (Or, maybe the *only* eastern and western Shaker you will ever see.)

The furniture, itself, is fascinating if you're into that sort of thing, but the story of how it got to the Golden Lamb is even better. Golden Lamb manager Jack Reynolds was visiting owner Robert Jones at his home in Lebanon one day when he spotted some furniture, covered up with heavy canvas drop cloths, in the garage. Removing the cloths, Reynolds found priceless Shaker pieces that Jones and his wife Virginia had collected but had no room to display. Jack quickly carved out some space in the unused rooms on the fourth floor of the Golden Lamb and created two of the hotel's most popular displays. Because of the unique and fragile nature of these pieces, they are kept behind glass and a locked door. Anyone wanting to examine this furniture up close must be accompanied by a member of management.

Time for another story.

One Friday, Jack Reynolds informed me that a noted Shaker devotee and author was going to be spending the night and wanted to see the furniture in the display rooms after dinner. Because I always worked late on Friday nights, I was elected to baby-sit the guest. I didn't see him when he checked in, but when he came down for dinner he was dressed in full Shaker garb, including a cape. The conversation was peppered with a lot of "thees" and "thous," and of course he had to sit in the Shaker Room, where he kept closing his eyes and breathing deeply throughout the meal.

After dinner, I dutifully retrieved the keys to the two display rooms and accompanied our guest to the fourth floor to get up close and personal with our stuff. We had to stop for about five minutes on the third floor landing so he could "prepare for my experience."

Now it really gets freaky.

Upon entering each room, our learned guest rubbed his hands all over the furniture. He rubbed up against the furniture. He opened cabinet drawers. He stuck his head inside the drawers and took a deep breath, as if to inhale the spirit of some long gone Shaker. Finally, after about ten very uncomfortable minutes on my part, he apparently had drunk in enough Shaker for one night and retreated to his room, where he no doubt spent the night dreaming of all the crazy times in Sabbathday Lake (a Shaker village in New Gloucester, Maine) 150 years ago.

Like I said, people get freaky around that stuff.

Though not as evident today, a lot of authentic Shaker foods were featured on the Golden Lamb menu during the "golden years" from 1973 to 1994. Guests could daily feast on Sister Lizzie's Shaker Sugar Pie, Brother Ricardo's Favorite Chicken Pudding, Sister Abigail's Blue Flower Omelet, Creamed Shaker Winter Cabbage, Hot Shaker Chicken Salad and Shaker Cider Chicken. And in answer to numerous inquiries over the years, there was indeed a Sister Lizzie, and a Brother Ricardo, and a Sister Abigail. Our chef, Erwin Pfeil, was a veritable expert on Shaker preparation and cuisine.

So there you have it . . . enough Shaker history to impress your friends the next time you come for dinner. True Shaker enthusiasts are probably wringing their hands and ready to burn the book right now, due to my lack of reverence for Mother Ann and her crew. But as said, if there were Shakers left in Lebanon today, I still think their attitude would be, "What's the big deal? It's only a chair."

well, some people might call it reindeer
Christmas at the Golden Lamb

Every year around the 18th of December I would be knee-deep into the Christmas season, grinding it out one day at a time and dreaming about that magical date, January 2, when everything would return to normal. The decorations, which looked so perfect on December 1, were now a little haggard, just like the employees. I was into my third week of herding a thousand people a day through the Golden Lamb, eating maybe one meal a day if I was lucky, fueling myself with nicotine, adrenalin and an invigorating coffee that the servers brewed called Double Joe. I was seeing my kids for a couple of hours, maybe two evenings a week, and sleeping all day on my one day off. The lobby filled up at eleven o'clock in the morning, and I didn't see the color of the carpet again until nine o'clock that night. I kept a calendar on my wall with the days in reverse, starting at December 31, so I could tell at a glance how many days were left in what seemed like a never-ending month.

Joe Emmet Christmas card

And then it happened. Some little old lady out for her annual Christmas lunch with "the girls," wearing her holiday sweatshirt, sitting beside a pile of gifts that, by the time they were opened, put me thirty minutes behind on my one o'clock turn, would flag me down as I was running madly through the dining room and say, "It must be really fun to work in a place like this at Christmas."

Madam . . . you have no idea.

This chapter should be long. Maybe it will be. Or maybe halfway through, I'll get tired of re-living those truly excruciating holiday seasons and just stop. Nevertheless, I keep asking myself the same question. How did any of us ever live to tell the tale?

For those of you who never experienced "Ohio's Oldest Inn" at Christmas during the golden years of 1973-1993, let me offer a few statistics. On average, we served over one thousand people a day—and even more on Saturdays, Sundays, and Christmas Eve. We changed decorations every year. We created special menus for lunch and dinner, and changed those menus every week. We had all the decorations up by December 1, and took them all down in a single day (December 31). We staged special celebrations that were featured in national publications (twice), and we became every television station's go-to location for a warm and fuzzy Christmas story. During my twenty-one holidays, we served over 600,000 people, and at times I feel like

I handed menus to every one of them. Again, I'm asking myself, How did we ever live through it?

When Jack Reynolds came to the Golden Lamb in July of 1969, December was one of the slowest months of the year for the restaurant and hotel. During the holidays, people were busy with shopping, office parties, holiday parties, and traveling, and therefore weren't coming out to dinner. At least that was the excuse. Jack, though, once told me he took one look around and asked himself, "How can a place that had Charles Dickens as a guest not be busy during the holidays?" During his twenty-five-year tenure as manager, Jack Reynolds would build a behemoth of a holiday celebration, one that started on Thanksgiving Day and lasted until January 2. And forty years later, his traditions and innovations continue to bring people into the Golden Lamb over the holidays.

It all began in February. The first week of the month, after we'd all caught our breath from the previous year's celebration, we sat down for what was to be the first of many "theme meetings." Every year, Christmas revolved around a theme, supported by decorations, meals, a Christmas card, promotional materials, signage, and so on. Carrying out the theme was the easy part; deciding what the theme would be, not so easy.

We all pitched our ideas. Some made it to Christmas; most never got beyond the talking stages. Themes usually revolved around whatever was hot on the antique or collectible circuit that year. But whatever we finally decided upon, it had to be traditional, it had to be somewhat "country," and we had to be able to support it with decorations either purchased or handmade.

When quilts were hot, we did quilts. When dolls were fashionable, we did dolls. When people were collecting candy molds and cookie cutters, we did "We're Molding A Merry Christmas At the Golden Lamb". (Don't ask me why.) One year, pottery was popular on the antique circuit and Jack Reynolds suggested the theme "Christmas Is A Crock". (That one, obviously, didn't make it.) Another year, someone suggested doing all edible decorations. We envisioned popcorn strings, cranberry garlands, candy on the tree, and lots of cookies and sugar ornaments. The tag-line was going to be "The Incredible Edible Christmas". But after running it by several people, we were convinced the National Egg Council might not like us borrowing a phrase they had spent millions of dollars developing. (So that one stayed in the box, too.)

Once the theme was established, it was up to me to "sell it" with a clever catch-phrase and a promotional brochure, which always debuted on Thanksgiving Day. The year we did dolls, it was easy: "We're All Dolled Up For Christmas At the Golden Lamb". The bicentennial

Bobby Taylor painting

year was a no-brainer: "The Christmas Spirit of '76 At the Golden Lamb." The year of the quilts, it was: "Christmas Is A Comfort At the Golden Lamb". That one practically wrote itself. But how do you tie in needlework samplers (which were hot one year) to Christmas? Well, you invite guests to "Enjoy A Christmas Sampler At the Golden Lamb". Get it? The play on words . . . sampler and sampler? OK, it wasn't one of my favorites either.

An ornament always helped sell the theme. We displayed the theme ornament on the Christmas tree in our lobby, one of five live trees we lugged in and out of the hotel every year. For our "White Christmas", we had hundreds of crocheted snowflakes decorating the lobby tree and the window wreaths. For "Christmas Is A Comfort", we used quilt blocks. The year of "Molding A Merry Christmas", Jack got white chocolate ornaments (made from the molds on the tree) to display in the lobby case. The ornaments looked great, but they brought a whole new crowd to the hotel that season—ants. We had to spray the case throughout the holidays to keep out the unwanted visitors.

One of the most memorable decorations was conceived for the Golden Lamb's "Christmas Spirit of '76", celebrating the nation's bicentennial. Jack had discovered an illustration by noted American artist Thomas Nast entitled, *Santa Claus In Camp*. Nast, an unabashed patriot, depicted Santa in a Union camp during the Civil War. But instead of wearing his fur-trimmed garb, St. Nick was dressed in a very patriotic star-spangled jacket and striped trousers. Quickly figuring out a way to capitalize on Jack's find, our intrepid decorator and jack-of-all-trades, Lani Stivers, got out her jigsaw and went to work. Lani reproduced colorful two-dimensional, hand-painted, red, white and blue Santas to hang on the hotel's tree, the chandeliers, the window wreaths and anywhere else we could find to put them. While she was at it, Lani made a few extras to sell in the gift shop. They sold out the first day. Then they started disappearing from the tree and the chandeliers. If I had a nickel for every one of those "Star-Spangled Santas" we could have sold, I wouldn't be sitting here writing this book.

Perhaps now is as good a time as any to talk about how we decorated for the Christmas holiday season at the Golden Lamb. Most people, when they think of Christmas, think primarily of two colors: red and green. A few might throw in a little burgundy here and there, maybe some gold. We didn't think that way. For over twenty years, we decorated for Christmas in every color imaginable and managed to sell it to the public. For "Christmas Spirit of '76", we did everything in red, white and blue, and it worked. For an early Christmas celebration called "Warmth of Christmas Past", we used gray and red. People bought it. For "We're Weaving A Homespun Christmas", it was blue, very light blue. For "Celebrate The Santa Season", it was all red, lots and lots of red. The year we did "We're All Dolled Up For Christmas", we used a lot of purple. Remarkably, our color schemes always worked. We did such a great job of selling the concept that no matter what we came up with, people bought it. They bought it because we were the Golden Lamb, and if we did it, it must be great.

Most of the celebrations are a blur now, but several still stand out, even after twenty years. In 1976, the theme was "We're Weaving A Homespun Christmas At the Golden Lamb". (We had done "Christmas Spirit of '76" the prior year.) Jack Reynolds and his wife Sandy had found an entire collection of late nineteenth-century and early twentieth-century shuttles, spools and weaving paraphernalia. The plan was to use them as decorations for that year's Christmas. It was a beautiful celebration, but I'll always remember it as the year we spent way, way too much money.

We picked out a piece of homespun material to use for the decorative bows and as a background for our special weekly menus, dessert menus, Christmas Eve menus, and on signage. Our long-time friend Skip Merten of Merten Printing Company, (who could take anything I gave him and make it look beautiful), photographed an actual homespun piece and reproduced it on card stock for our menus.

We also got the bright idea to have a lamb and wreath embossed on all of our printed material. Throughout the process, Skip kept hinting to me that it wasn't going to be inexpensive. First, the dye had to be made. And a second press run would be necessary, with heavier stock to take the embossing.

"Sure you want to do this?" Skip asked.

When the menus and brochures arrived a few days before Thanksgiving, we were thrilled. The homespun effect was perfect. The blind embossing gave the menus a rich and elegant look. They were probably the most beautiful menus we had ever produced. We always had a difficult time keeping our holiday menus because everyone wanted a set as a souvenir. We printed extras, knowing some were going to walk out the door. But this particular season, they started disappearing faster than normal. Then came January, and we got the bill. For the weekly menus, dessert menus, and brochures, the cost was over $5,000. Typically, we spent less than $2,000. Needless to say, in the future we kept our embossing and extra press runs to a minimum. But as I said, they were beautiful menus.

I can't finish this story without an appreciative nod to Skip Merten and his company. For over twenty years, he and his staff at Merten Printing produced all of the extravagant holiday materials for the Golden Lamb. No matter what we wanted or how late we brought something in, Skip always managed to get it to us by our 11 a.m. deadline on Thanksgiving Day. I remember one Thanksgiving in particular when Skip and his toddler twin sons delivered brochures to us early in the morning, just in time for the beginning of the holiday season. The full color reproductions of the hotel's Christmas cards, produced by Merten Company, are still sold in the gift shop, and the early prints sought-after by collectors of Golden Lamb memorabilia.

While almost all of our Christmas celebrations were highly successful, a few, unfortunately, didn't hit the mark. We thought we were pretty clever the year we got "All Dolled Up For Christmas", using dolls and doll heads for decorations. We also decided we weren't going to use just any dolls or doll heads. Oh no. We found a source for reproduction nineteenth-century porcelain doll heads in three sizes, which we displayed on the tree, in the wreaths, and on the hotel's chandeliers. Someone even suggested doing a mantle display with various sizes and styles of doll heads tucked in the greenery. But we found out, much to our chagrin, that young children weren't too excited about seeing all those disembodied heads hanging from the Christmas tree. And the generations of little girls who grew up with Barbie didn't quite understand why the hair was painted on, the faces were stark white, and the lips were bright red. So much for our clever idea.

Remember in the early 1980s when depictions of watermelons and watermelon slices were big on the primitive and folk art decorating circuit? Well, in 1982 they got kicked aside (for awhile) by hearts. Anyone into folk art decorating, had hearts of all shapes and sizes throughout their homes. Always willing to exploit a trend (no matter how brief), we celebrated "A Hearty Country Christmas At the Golden Lamb" in December of 1982 with hearts on the tree and hearts hanging from the chandeliers. We even had special wooden, heart-shaped candle holders made for all the tables. I can't remember what illustration I used that year to sell the concept, but whatever it was, it didn't work. After enduring thirty-one days of "Is it Valentine's Day already?" jokes, we packed our hearts away and once again waited for next year.

Twice, the first time in 1981 and then again in 1990, the Golden Lamb's holiday theme was "We're Having A Dickens' of A Christmas At the Golden Lamb". If we knew one thing, it was that the public could never get enough of our famous English guest. With lots of polished brass, copper, and burgundy velvet, the hotel looked like a Victorian country inn. We already had the Dickens Carolers, who performed every year, and two Dickens rooms. During the first celebration in 1981, we introduced one of our most popular holiday meals, "Cratchet's Christmas Dinner," and a new holiday beverage, "Smoking

Bishop" (taken from Charles Dickens's own recipe).

And while we're talking about food . . . The decorations may have been the driving force behind holidays at the Golden Lamb, but the food wasn't far behind. We always dressed up the menu at Christmas with different lunch and dinner items, a completely new dessert menu, and, of course, higher prices. We usually had one price increase a year, done right before the busiest month.

In my early years, the Golden Lamb presented a holiday extravaganza called "The Holiday Buffet of Many Lands". Chef Erwin Pfeil pulled out all the stops for this once-a-year culinary happening, drawing upon his extensive European training not only for the exotic menu items but the displays as well. The buffet stretched from one end of the Lebanon Room to the other, and there wasn't a turkey, Swiss steak, or piece of fried chicken in sight. We had two seatings only and always sold out within days of the tickets becoming available. My only memories are of cracking open a bottle of champagne when the last guest made it through the line, although I was too young to have any of the bubbly. "The Holiday Buffet of Many Lands" was a short-lived tradition, lasting only three years. By 1973, the Golden Lamb had become increasingly busy over the holidays and there just wasn't enough time for such a labor-intensive feast.

For Christmas of 1973, we established our routine of special weekly menus featuring venison, goose, and turkey. Two years later, with the addition of our Mount Vernon menu, we established a set of menus that have lasted until this day.

The first week in December always features venison in a menu created by our great former chef, Erwin Pfeil. "FroheWeihachten" was Chef Pfeil's signature meal, which drew heavily upon his German heritage and European Christmas traditions. Jokingly referred to around the hotel as "The Bambi Buffet," the meal featured sautéed medallions of Venison St. Hubert, celery root salad, braised red cabbage, potato croquettes and our own Black Forrest Yule Log for dessert. And for twenty-one years, Chef Pfeil personally sautéed every order of venison served to a guest. By the end of the first week, his right wrist was shot and the rest of his arm wasn't much better.

Venison is one of those foods everyone has heard about but most people haven't actually tasted. Or, if they had tasted venison, it probably spent too many months in someone's freezer and wasn't the cut or quality we prepared. Venison, particularly in the large quantities we used, isn't something that's readily available. We ordered ours in June or July for a late November delivery from the Cinnabar Game Farm in Paradise Valley, Montana, and therein lies a tale.

In the late 1970s, the National Restaurant Association put on a big push for a program called "Truth In Menu." Apparently more than a few restaurants were playing fast and loose with the descriptions of their menu items, using a few adjectives where they didn't belong. So the Restaurant Association began encouraging owners and operators to be careful about what adjectives they used on their menus. If a menu said baked Idaho potato, there had better be a box from Boise in the storeroom. If a menu listed fresh fish, it had better never been frozen. The Golden Lamb always advertised a product correctly because we had nothing to hide. If we said fresh fish, it was. If we said something was made from scratch, we were always glad to show you the recipe. We even changed our Prime Rib of Beef to Standing Rib of Beef because our ribs weren't prime grade but choice grade, as is 90 percent of the beef rib served in restaurants today. So if you ever wondered why the Golden Lamb doesn't serve prime rib . . . there's your answer.

The same year we re-worded the description of our ribs, we made our usual summer call to Welch Brogan at the Cinnabar Game Farm to order venison for the coming holiday season. Only this time, Welch was a little hesitant on the phone. He wasn't sure if he could fill our entire Christmas season order. Brogan admitted that for years he had hunted some deer himself but also had been buying lots of venison from the state of Montana. If a buck had been shot out of season or escaped into an area where it had to be shot by authorities, Welch was always there, checkbook in hand. The venison was fine, perfectly delicious in fact. The popularity of the meal proved that. But in my mind, the romantic image of a hunter surviving off of wild game quickly disappeared.

The truth was, as Welch told me, Montana had tightened up its game laws, and confiscated bucks were no longer sold. This left the Golden Lamb and the Cinnabar Game Farm high and dry.

But Brogan had a solution.

"I can get you some Alaskan venison," he said. "All you want."

"Alaskan venison?" I said. "I've never heard of that before. What is it?"

"Well . . . they grow them up there in . . . uh . . . herds, yeah herds. Kind of like sheep or cattle."

Truth in Menu reared its ugly head.

"Uh, Welch," I said, "would you call those reindeer?"

"Well, some people might call it reindeer," he offered weakly.

"Would most people call it reindeer?" I shot back.

"Well, yes," Brogan said. "If you have to put a name on it, yeah, it's reindeer."

I immediately visualized pickets in front of the Golden Lamb, and hordes of crying little kids, when we advertised that we were serving Rudolph on the Christmas menu. I was fully prepared to tell them it wasn't Rudolph . . . it was Prancer.

We scrambled and found another supplier. Fortunately, a purveyor in Kansas City had a supply with the correct pedigree, which we purchased for that year only. By the following year, Welch Brogan had gotten back on track as our supplier and we enjoyed a long association, buying not only venison but also elk for our "Bounty of Harvest" celebration in early November.

For the second week in December, we always prepared goose, another one of those traditional foods everyone had heard about but few had ever tried. In the early years, we took that poor goose all over the world trying to find the correct spot for it. One year it was an American meal, the next year an English meal, the next a "traditional" Ohio meal . . . One year we even moved it to Sweden! We could never find anyone from outside the United States who ate goose for Christmas. We kept asking foreign guests the same question, "What do you eat for Christmas dinner?" And we kept getting the same answer, turkey!

Early dessert menu

We polled guests from France, Germany, England, Canada, and Spain, among other places, trying to find a permanent home for our goose. Trying to find somebody . . . anybody . . . who would admit to eating goose every year at Christmas. We never found one.

Finally, in 1976, we introduced "Cratchet's Christmas Dinner" with a menu supplied by our old friend Charles Dickens. The menu first appeared in 1843 in Dickens's classic novel, *A Christmas Carol*. It included roast goose with stuffing, a salad from Camden town (a totally made-up name that worked), mashed potatoes and a Dickens' of a plum pudding.

For the holiday season, the bakery started making plum puddings in early November. We used a traditional recipe with an ingredient list that was a full-page long, typewritten, and single-spaced. Every time I read the recipe, I thought to myself: Do Not Try This At Home. I passed it out to more than a few people, knowing full well they wouldn't have the nerve to attempt it.

Once the puddings were made, they had to be "seasoned." Seasoning involved wrapping the puddings in brandy-soaked clothes and storing them in large, covered plastic containers for about a month. The brandy was replenished at regular intervals until the puddings were ripe and ready to serve. Add a little harde sauce (made with more rum or brandy) and you had a dessert that was attractive, traditional and alcoholic all at the same time. It was a win-win-win situation.

One year I decided to serve the puddings flaming (ala Dickens) to guests in the private party rooms. Unfortunately, nobody told me that you had to warm the brandy in order to get it to ignite. I poured enough brandy on my first plum puddings that by the time the bottle was empty, the guests knew that any missing pyrotechnics would be more than made up for by sheer alcohol.

I never was a big fan of plum pudding. Judging by the amount that came back half-eaten, we didn't make a lot of fans with it either. We served thousands of plum pudding desserts throughout the holiday seasons. Notice I said "served." I don't know how many actually were eaten. I vividly remember lots of school groups, in an effort to expose their students to traditional holiday fare, pre-ordering plum pudding for a dessert. One bite, though, and it was all over. History notwithstanding, the kids would much rather have had ice cream. Me too.

The Golden Lamb's menu for the third week of December—turkey and Virginia ham—first appeared in the early 1970s. In 1975, it became "Christmas at Mount Vernon," the first of our bicentennial menus that were served January through March of 1976. For this menu, Jack Reynolds coined a phrase that stood us well for over twenty years. We always shied away from using the word "authentic" when describing menus or menu items. During the course of our research (and we did lots of research), we discovered that if a recipe was truly authentic, it probably wasn't very good. And if a recipe was good, it probably wasn't authentic. Sound strange? Read on.

In preparing truly authentic recipes, we quickly discovered that many of them would not be palatable to the dining public of the twentieth century. When these recipes were created, people lived entirely different lifestyles than the guests we served day in and day out. Our ancestors did more physical labor. They didn't have the benefits of central heating and cooling. They lacked refrigeration and any way of adequately preserving food. They ate a lot more carbohydrates, used more sugar, and a heck of a lot more salt. So if we produced these recipes "authentically," most of our guests wouldn't have eaten the food. And who's to say what Charles Dickens, Martin Van Buren or George Washington actually ate?

In order to keep us legitimate, Jack came up with the phrase "foods typical of the times," meaning foods available during a particular era. We didn't say George Washington or Martin Van Buren or Mark Twain actually did eat this or that, but they certainly could have. For almost twenty-five years, the Golden Lamb had only three "authentic" menus, and they were taken from previously published sources. The first was the "Dickens Christmas" meal that came right out of the book. The second was "Christmas at Mount Vernon," a menu of items supposedly served at George Washington's country estate in Virginia. The third was a menu served in February of 1976 for a meal honoring Mark Twain as part of our bicentennial series. It came from Twain's book, *A Tramp Abroad*, and listed a lengthy series of items he wished served "immediately upon his arrival from Europe."

Desserts were always a big hit during December. We served the same menu every day (instead of changing dessert menus every day like we did the rest of the year), but we doubled the number of offerings and, of course, raised prices. Old standbys were Sister Lizzie's Shaker Sugar Pie, Golden Lamb cheesecake and pumpkin pie. We also added ambrosia, plum puddings, mincemeat pie, peppermint ice cream pie with chocolate sauce, something made with pecans (either pies or tarts), and a very versatile dessert we called Golden Lamb Yule Log.

Golden Lamb Yule Log was a dense spice cake made from a recipe we found . . . somewhere. Baked in a loaf pan, it was sliced off and served with traditional hot rum sauce, which was no more than powdered sugar, water and a little bit of rum for flavor. But what's interesting is that throughout the month of December in the downstairs dining rooms, it was called Christmas Eve Pudding.

Upstairs (in the private party rooms), it was Golden Lamb Yule Log. And on Thanksgiving and during our two-week "Bounty of Harvest" celebration in November, it was Harvest Pudding. We served the very same dessert under three different names (and sometimes with three different prices) and in the thirty-five years I was there . . . and nobody caught on.

Ambrosia was a traditional southern dessert featuring citrus fruit and coconut. Citrus fruits and coconut appeared only around the holidays in the nineteenth century, due to a lack of refrigeration and mass transportation. They were considered special treats that were never readily available year-round. I remember my grandfather and grandmother always putting an orange or two in my Christmas stocking. As a child, of course, I never understood the historical significance. I only knew it wasn't candy. Apparently patrons in the 1970s didn't understand the historical importance either, because ambrosia didn't exactly fly off the shelves during lunch and dinner. Somewhere along the way, we dumped it and started serving pistachio ice cream. So much for tradition.

There was always a little drinking during the holidays and, in fact, we encouraged it. Jack found a great recipe for traditional English wassail. Please notice I didn't say authentic English wassail. If you search through enough cookbooks, you'll probably find enough wassail recipes to fill, well, a cookbook. The range of ingredients includes cranberry juice, pineapple juice, apple juice, apple cider, whole apples, and baked apples. Our recipe was pretty basic, and what I liked about it was that it was almost pure alcohol, including brandy, sherry, sugar, a little water, and spices. We started serving the popular punch to private parties, only on demand. When they demanded it, we usually had to make a quick run to Eddie Kilpatrick's carryout on Sycamore Street to pick up a few bottles of the least expensive brandy and sherry we could find. (When the alcohol was mixed with sugar and all those spices, it

certainly didn't pay to buy the good stuff.) One holiday season, when wassail proved particularly popular, Eddie asked me point-blank, "What are you using all this cheap stuff for?" I lied and told him we were cooking with it.

Over the years, the batches of our holiday wassail got larger and larger. We were making eight to ten gallons of the punch, several times a week. At the height of the holiday celebrations during the

We're Having A Dickens' Of A Christmas At The Golden Lamb

'A CHRISTMAS CAROL'

SCROOGE AND BOB CRATCHIT AND A BOWL OF SMOKING BISHOP

Dickens' of a Christmas menu

1970s and 1980s, we were burning through brandy and sherry at the rate of thirty cases per week. Somehow I became the wassail expert, and it was my job to produce the product. Dutifully, about three times a week, I'd assemble ingredients in the kitchen, round up the largest pot I could find, and set to work. In went the sherry, the brandy, sugar by the pound, water by the quart and lots of spices, including whole cloves, whole allspice, stick cinnamon, ground nutmeg and ground ginger. Then it was just a matter of standing by the stove and watching it heat. Walking away wasn't an option, because if the mixture got too hot, it tended to catch on fire. The recipe made about ten gallons, enough to last about three days.

The other famous holiday cocktail at the Golden Lamb was a wonderful concoction called "Smoking Bishop". The drink is mentioned in *A Christmas Carol* when Ebenezer Scrooge talks about celebrating the holidays "with a bowl of Smoking Bishop." It was an interesting name and sounded traditional. Notice I didn't say authentic. I found a pretty good recipe in the book *Drinking with Dickens*, written by Cedric Charles Dickens, a distant relative of the great author himself. The recipe was straightforward, having only four ingredients. But one of those ingredients was described as "good Portuguese red wine." The only Portuguese red wine I could find was far too expensive and far too good to be heated up with the other ingredients.

Our good friend and wine merchant, Mike Monnin, came to the rescue. When I explained to him what I needed, Mike said he had just the thing. When he quoted the price, my first question was, "Does it come in a bottle or a fifty-gallon drum?" Who knew you could get really good wine from . . . Yugoslavia? And in this case, like all the others, he didn't let me down. The wine turned out to be terrific and another Golden Lamb holiday tradition was born. Only now I had two pots to watch on the stove.

On the subject of drinks, let's not forget that holiday favorite, "Golden Lamb Egg Nog". We served it at dinner time, Monday through Friday, in a punch bowl in the lobby. This was another one of those beverages mixed in bulk. We started out serving our egg nog in glass punch cups, but quickly ditched the glass cups in favor of disposable plastic ones, much to the delight of the dishwasher. For years we kept the recipe a secret in order to enhance the traditional feeling and, quite frankly, make ourselves look good. But after all these years, let's tell the truth. The Golden Lamb's signature egg nog was a commercial brand, purchased in half-gallon containers and spiced up with extra whipped cream and nutmeg on the top. We made it up in five-gallon buckets. So much for authentic or traditional.

Our holiday displays were always a big part of the seasonal celebrations. Every year we tried to present something new that was also traditional (not that easy to do, when you think about it). Some displays lasted only a year. Some gained a permanent spot in the yearly extravaganza. In the early years, we changed displays every week and included demonstrations on everything from wrapping packages to decorating Christmas cookies. But as we got busier and busier, the extras started quickly dropping by the wayside due to lack of time and space.

One of the most impressive displays was the "'Twas the Night Before Christmas" Room, a re-creation of the Clement Clarke Moore's famous 1822 poem, also titled *A Visit From St. Nicholas*. The display was set up on the second floor in the Vallandigham (Dining) Room that we redecorated as a child's bedroom, with a small single antique bed, an old fashioned-looking Christmas tree, and some period toys and decorations. We even got a mannequin (sort of) to put in the bed to give the appearance of a child sleeping. But the centerpiece was a wingback chair in which Santa Claus appeared to be seated. The chair faced away from the doorway so that all anyone could see was the top of Santa's head and an arm draped casually over the edge of the chair. To adults it looked just like what it was. But to kids it was magic. (Dining room space became too valuable, so we eventually had to move Santa down the hall to Room 31, where he stayed for almost two decades until the bedroom revenue became too valuable to give up for a month. Scores of guests asked about Santa in his chair, but unlike the music box, this tradition unfortunately never returned.)

Everybody loved the "'Twas the Night Before Christmas" Room—even I liked it, and I was never big on Christmas. It was a cute display. Then Jack decided the children should be able to hear Moore's poem as well. The job fell to me to make it happen. After more than a few phone calls, I found a continuous loop tape recorder and we mounted a switch about three feet off the floor, just the right height for a child to push the button. We got Elva Adams, director of the Warren County Historical Society, to do the reading. I even hauled the Regina music box up to the second floor so we could have a tinkling "Jingle Bells" playing in the background. With edits, the finished recording was three minutes long. We discovered, however, that the attention span of our younger guests seemed to diminish after about sixty seconds, apparently due to the sugar high they had achieved by drinking too much egg nog and eating too much peppermint ice cream pie. So the recording had to be shortened. Again, it was up to me to perform the miracle of Christmas. Elva wasn't available, so I took the recorder home over the weekend. I had the presence of mind to pre-record "Jingle Bells" playing on the Regina music box, and after about thirty attempts and some serious editing was able to come up with a 59-second version of the poem. My kids heard it so many times, they got burnt out on it for life. To this day, my oldest daughter, Alexandra, remembers that fateful weekend when all I did was spout "'Twas the Night Before Christmas."

Our "Chicken Feather Christmas Tree" was always a favorite display of guests at the inn. This unique decoration, displayed behind glass, occupied a corner of the lobby for over two decades. The large tree (circa 1900) was really made out of chicken feathers (a fact many guests refused to believe). They thought artificial trees were a product of the 1960s, remembering those tin foil monstrosities with the revolving light that shown from below and turned the tree different colors. And don't forget, all the ornaments had to be the same size, shape, and color. But long before those artificial trees made their thankfully brief appearance on the holiday scene, Americans were making trees out of feathers. Dyed green and wrapped around flexible wires, the feathers strangely resembled pine needles.

Christmas trees, as a popular custom, didn't catch on in this country until the late 1800s. The typical feather tree stood on a tabletop and was three to four feet high. Somehow, somewhere, Jack and Sandy Reynolds found an authentic floor-standing feather tree that topped out at about six feet. During some part of its history, it had been "hard wired" with lights. This meant that the light sockets and wires were permanent parts of the tree. There were four strings of lights with eight lights per string connected in a series. If one light went out, all eight lights went out. And they went out quite often. And whose job was it to see the lights stayed on? You guessed it.

The lights, themselves, were a particular problem in that they hadn't been manufactured in over twenty-five years. Every year we made a plea for more lights, asking guests to check their attics, basements, and garages for bulbs they no longer used. One year a guest brought in three boxes of "brand new" lights. Closer examination, however, showed they were "brand new" in 1960. The lights supposedly were discovered on the top shelf of a local hardware store, where they were covered with dust and still bearing the original price tag of forty-nine cents. But they worked!

The spectacular collection of period ornaments decorating the feather tree were lovingly collected throughout the years by Jack and Sandy Reynolds, with a few added each year. Most of the ornaments were blown glass or paper, dating from the 1920s, '30s, and '40s. My favorites were a set of plastic birds, probably from the '40s, that balanced perfectly on any branch due to the lead weights in their long, flowing tails. The silver dirigibles and silver glass balls also were striking ornaments, both of which were much heavier than anything made today. Because of their value, the period ornaments were wrapped in tissue paper, placed in individual sections of large cardboard boxes, and stored separately from the other decorations. Each year we carefully unpacked them the last week of November and then carefully re-packed them the first week of January. Between packing and unpacking, we spent much of our time convincing guests that "yes, the tree really is made out of chicken feathers."

The Golden Lamb was lucky over the years in finding different displays for the Christmas season. We were always amazed by the generosity of our guests, who graciously loaned us their collections for display in the big apothecary case we hauled in for the holiday season and put in the lobby. Look at it this way. If you were a collector of Christmas antiques and memorabilia, when would you want to display these in your own home? Maybe at Christmas?

I particularly remember a collection of fragile Dresden Christmas ornaments. These intricate ornaments, made entirely of paper and cardboard, were produced in Dresden, Germany, between 1890 and 1910. Traditional holiday shapes were present along with animal shapes, which were also popular. The collection included only fourteen items, but their pristine condition and intricate designs made for a memorable display. The only thing more stunning than the ornaments was the bill we received in January for thirty-two days of extra insurance coverage for the antique ornaments. Who knew paper was worth so much?

One year our good friends and long-time guests, Larry and Carol Fobiano, loaned us their Christmas miniatures. These intricate and spectacular miniature scenes were made for Larry's even more intricate and spectacular train collection. He had constructed the Golden Lamb, the old Albee Theater in Cincinnati, and various storefronts in downtown Lebanon, including the Village Ice Cream Parlor. The miniature buildings, each standing about three feet tall, were fully illuminated and exact in every detail. The Golden Lamb miniature even replicated the wavy nineteenth-century glass in the front lobby windows and the 1930s tile on the lobby floor.

Over the years we were loaned a collection of early *Saturday Evening Post* Christmas covers (compliments of Curtis Publishing), a large collection of antique Shaker tinware (compliments of Mr. and Mrs. Robert Jones), fine collection of painted toleware (thanks to good friend Marvin Bishop), a nostalgic collection of early children's toys (Marilyn Hailey came through for us again), and the most intricate, fully furnished dollhouse I have ever seen (compliments of Sandy Reynolds).

Some years we came up with our own displays. The year of "Christmas Is A Comfort", the quilts submitted for the contest became the focal display. (We should have bought more of those.) The year we did "Enjoy A Christmas Sampler", the submitted holiday samplers for our contest filled the lobby. (We should have bought more of those, too.)

Other displays, like the "'Twas the Night Before Christmas" Room and the feather tree, became staples of the yearly celebration. For a number of years we had a revolving musical German Christmas tree stand displayed at the front desk. Jack found it at an antique shop during the early 1980s and bought it, even though it didn't work. It was an intricate piece of machinery with inner workings more complicated than a clock. There was a spring-wound motor with lots of small and large gears and a set of miniature bells, each with an individual striker. None of us had ever seen anything like it. The motor would spin a small tabletop size tree and music would play. But remember, ours didn't work. Somehow . . . somewhere Jack Reynolds found someone who could repair a revolving German musical Christmas tree stand. When it was returned to us, just in time for Christmas, we set it up by the front desk, wound it up and waited. Slowly the tree started to revolve and a tinkling rendition of "Jingle Bells" came forth. After the song stopped, we heard a series of notes that made no sense whatsoever. It took us until the end of the month to realize what we were hearing was "Jingle Bells," backwards, as the mechanism rewound.

In early 1983, Jack found a mechanical Santa's workshop, which he was sure was going to be the hit of the season. I had never seen him so excited about a "find." The glass display case was about three feet tall and four feet long, and probably dated from the 1920s or '30s. It held a miniature Santa's workshop complete with elves. Run by an electric motor, the elves traveled across the workshop on a type of treadmill carrying toys, only to disappear into a paper mache mountainside and then reappear on the other side to start the whole process over again. The display was in excellent condition: original glass, no damage to the case, all the elves intact. The only problem, of course, was that it didn't work.

Jack took the display home and set up his own Santa's workshop in the garage. He commandeered the services of our maintenance man, Marlowe Rich, for a complete rebuild. They disassembled the entire display, repaired the motor, made new belts and pulleys, and after several frustrating weeks finally got the thing up and running. We placed it on the second floor at the head of the stairs for our "Celebrate The Santa Season" in 1983. For an entire month, the troupe of elves glided through the workshop, carrying their toys, disappearing into the mountainside, and then reappearing to start again. And nobody said a word. Apparently our guests weren't as impressed with Jack's find as he was. Maybe a piece from the twentieth century wasn't old enough to get people excited at the Golden Lamb. Maybe, like me, the guests thought the elf dressed in white looked too much like Elvis to be taken seriously. Maybe people just didn't see it on the second floor. But after one Christmas season, Santa's workshop found a permanent home in the fourth floor storeroom, never to be seen again.

Because we still had a restaurant and hotel to run in the days before the holidays started, we always used outside decorators. Our first team of decorators (and the ones who set the standards for decades to come) were Nancy Dornetti and Nancy Dornetti. That's right. Nancy and Nancy were married to brothers. They came up with the idea of the big impact tree in the lobby, the fabric and greenery swags, wreaths in the windows, and those big bows that became such a part of our yearly celebrations. After a few years the Dornettis left us in the capable hands of Lani Stivers and Betty Carpenter, who helped the Golden Lamb gain national recognition for its Christmas celebrations during the late 1970s and all through the 1980s.

The schedule for decorating the hotel was never the same two years in a row. We didn't start decorating until the day after Thanksgiving and everything had to be hung and ready by December 1. Because the date for Thanksgiving changed each year, sometimes Lani and Betty had a week to decorate, sometimes as few as four days. But somehow they always got it done.

During the four to seven days for decorating, Lani and Betty lived at the hotel, literally. They usually stayed in Room 27 on the third floor so they would have plenty of space to spread out their decorations, many of which weren't even assembled until they actually started. Most of my memories of Lani Stivers and Betty Carpenter revolve around stepladders and bows. When I came to work at 7:30 in the morning, Lani would be perched high on a stepladder, hanging swags from the ceiling or decorations on a tree, while Betty kept a steady stream of decorations going up the ladder. Whenever I left at night—6:30, 8:30, 11:30—Lani would be on her ladder hanging bows that Betty, who was sitting on the floor, had just tied. Their decorating skills were featured in *Americana* magazine (on the cover), *Ford Times* magazine, numerous television news stories and more newspaper articles than you could count. Though we all pitched in to help, it was Lani and Betty who actually made it all happen.

The sequence of decorating was similar from year to year. The Dickens Bedroom and the "'Twas the Night Before Christmas" Room usually got done first. After those were decorated, we could close the doors until December 1. Next came the upstairs dining rooms, the downstairs dining rooms, and last but not least the lobby, which always held the theme tree. Many years, Lani and Betty decorated right up until the beginning of the lunch hour. But every year for more than two decades, we were ready to go by 11 o'clock in the morning on December 1. I'm certain our two decorators never slept the entire time they were there. They couldn't have. There was too much work to do.

On December 31, everything had to come down in a single day. It was our tradition that by 5 p.m. on New Year's Eve, the only vestige of Christmas left was the tree in the lobby, which had been totally un-decorated and then redecorated all in white for the new year. More than a few hotel guests were confused. When they checked in at 2 o'clock in the afternoon there was a Christmas tree in the lobby, and by the time they came down for dinner it was all white. Even now, after all these years, when I think about the fact that we had to un-decorate five live Christmas trees, nine dining rooms, the lobby, the bar, the hallways and the kids' Christmas room, I still wonder how it ever got done. Somehow, some way, it always did. Everything would be stripped, packed in garbage bags, tagged, and then hauled to the third- and fourth-floor storerooms to await next year's celebrations. The live trees (except for the lobby tree) were hauled out the door and raffled off to the employees. More than a few of those trees are still alive and thriving today.

There is a lot more that could be written about Christmas at the Golden Lamb. There are many stories to tell about Wayne and Georgia Dunn and their group, the Dickens Carolers. For those of you who never had the pleasure to hear them, and it was a great pleasure, the Dickens Carolers were a group of local residents who sang at the inn throughout the holidays. When they started in 1971, the carolers were all young adults who thought it would be fun to dress up in period costumes and sing throughout our dining rooms. By the time they finished their stint in 2000, we were giving them money for babysitters so they could make their performances.

Over the years the members of the group changed, but their popularity soared. Guests would call, wanting to make their reservations on the nights the carolers were going to sing. Because they were a totally volunteer group, we had to inform guests that we never knew when they were coming. They would just show up. The Dickens Carolers grew so popular that after a few years we asked them not to visit on Friday or Saturday nights, as their appearances tended to slow down the service. Even if guests were finished with dinner, nobody left the room when the carolers walked in.

In the private party rooms on the second floor, the Dickens Carolers were always a blessing. Private parties, by nature, tend not to run on time because they have a room booked for the whole night. Consequently, if the first party is thirty minutes late, it can throw the timing off for the whole evening. Many a night I'd meet Wayne or Georgia as they came up the stairs and whisper, "Buy me some time. Go to the Corwin Room first." Or, "Save the Presidents Room until last. They're drinking like crazy and I don't want to interrupt them."

Looking back on those holidays, I still wonder how we ever got it all done. From the day after Thanksgiving until January 2, it was a constant battle to maintain some type of order and discipline during thirty days of what we used to call "well-decorated chaos." The lobby always filled up at 11 o'clock in the morning and if we were lucky, we got a half-hour break in the afternoon. Then at 5 p.m., it started all over again.

I used to feel that Christmas at the Golden Lamb was a monster we created. We worked hard to build it, but once it came to life, we somehow lost control. No matter what happened, whether we increased prices, had a lousy economy, or crappy weather, we were always full. Every year it was a daily goal to do more: more than last year, more than last week, more than yesterday. At night I sometimes escaped the chaos and just stood out on the balcony in the dark, wondering just how much more could we do. And the answer always was . . . we could do more.

Jack Reynolds had the right attitude when it came to the crowds at the hotel. He would stare at the lobby full of people and say to me, "They ain't going away, so we'd better get them in."

More than a few people began to comment in the late '80s and early '90s that perhaps we were getting a little too commercial with our celebrations, that we had lost sight of being "an old fashioned country inn" by putting on these holiday extravaganzas every year. But every holiday season I'd see the same faces coming back for their annual dose of Christmas at the Golden Lamb. The same guests who complained about not being able to find a parking space, not being able to get the exact reservation time they wanted, not being able to get as large a table as they wanted, they kept coming back. So we must have been doing something right.

I still wonder how we survived. I think what kept us going, despite the stress and sheer exhaustion, was the fact that we were doing something that nobody else could do. We were giving guests things they just couldn't get anywhere else. We were the biggest, we were the most well-known, the hottest ticket in town, and we were damn proud of it. So today, if I ran into that little old lady in her Christmas sweatshirt, out for lunch with the girls, I'd have to say, "Yeah, it was great to work in a place like that." I just didn't realize it at the time.

Who Says The Tree Has to Be Green?

Twenty-Seven Years of Christmas At the Golden Lamb

1971   It's A Calico Christmas At the Golden Lamb

1972   You're Part Of The Melody Of Christmas At the Golden Lamb

1973   Natural-ly It's Christmas At the Golden Lamb

1974   Enjoy The Warmth Of Christmas Past At the Golden Lamb

1975   Celebrate The Christmas Spirit of '76 At the Golden Lamb

1976   We're Weaving A Homespun Christmas At the Golden Lamb

1977	Der Belschnickle and Kris Kringle, A German Country Christmas At the Golden Lamb
1978	Christmas Is A Comfort At the Golden Lamb
1979	We're Cooking Up A Merry Christmas At the Golden Lamb
1980	We're Having A White Christmas At the Golden Lamb
1981	We're Having A Dickens' Of A Christmas At the Golden Lamb
1982	Celebrate A Hearty Country Christmas At the Golden Lamb
1983	Celebrate The Santa Season At the Golden Lamb
1984	Celebrate A Star Spangled Christmas At the Golden Lamb
1985	It's Time For Christmas At the Golden Lamb
1986	Enjoy A Christmas Sampler At the Golden Lamb
1987	We're Molding A Merry Christmas At the Golden Lamb
1988	Enjoy A Sugar And Spice Christmas At the Golden Lamb
1989	It's A Frosty Country Christmas At the Golden Lamb
1990	We're Having A Dickens' Of A Christmas At the Golden Lamb (II)
1991	Nutcrackers, A Modern Christmas Tradition At The Golden Lamb
1992	We're All Dolled Up For Christmas At the Golden Lamb
1993	Celebrate the Golden Season At the Golden Lamb

1994   Christmas Lives At the Golden Lamb

1995   We're All Wrapped Up In Christmas At the Golden Lamb

1996   Celebrate A Child's Country Christmas At the Golden Lamb

1997   Celebrate A Winter Wonderland At the Golden Lamb

CENTRAL VIEW, LEBANON.   *Drawn by Henry Howe in 1846.*

Now you see it...then you didn't, a short course in Golden Lamb architecture

The Golden Lamb's four-story, Federal-style brick building with its three-story balcony (that doesn't really fit architecturally with the building) has been the subject of countless paintings and thousands of photographs, while serving as a landmark for almost two centuries. You can almost see old Jonas Seaman standing in front of the majestic hotel at the southwest corner of Main and Broadway streets in Lebanon, welcoming travelers and townspeople alike to share a table under the sign of the Golden Lamb.

Picture it all you want, it never happened.

Today's Golden Lamb is a far cry from Seaman's establishment. His tavern was a much smaller structure than what guests see today— much smaller. Over the course of 162 years, the hotel got bigger and bigger, attaining its present size in 1965. Along the way, it gained three floors, lost some stables by the side of the building, gained more basement space, lost some overnight rooms, and gained a parking lot, which is big but never big enough.

On August 19, 1803, Jonas Seaman took title to Lot 57 from Ichabod Corwin who, in today's terms, was the Donald Trump of his day. Cost of the lot was $67.50. Four months and one week later (on December 26), Seaman opened the doors to his sturdy, one-story log tavern. It was built back from the street because there were no sidewalks. Homes and businesses were usually constructed with a setback to allow wagons and horses plenty of room for passage over the dirt roads, which had no drainage.

Seaman's tavern occupied the site of what is now the Lebanon (Dining) Room. As you walk through the archway from the lobby, imagine a one-room structure that extended to the current tavern and gift shop section. It was just a little wider than the present-day dining room. There was, no doubt, a central fireplace in the rear of the tavern for cooking, and common tables in the front. Entrance was gained through a single door facing Broadway. And of course there was no bar.

There were no drawings or paintings of the inn, either, during this period. The earliest depiction of the Golden Lamb appeared in 1844, and by that time the building had three floors. So nobody is sure exactly what it looked like . . . which reminds me of a story.

One evening in 1975, a server came to me and said the words few restaurant operators like to hear. "The party having dinner in the Vallandigham Room would like to see you," she said. I immediately inquired if the party had gone well and was assured it had. The server even told me the group had tipped her well above the normal 15 percent. Everybody seemed happy.

I checked the reservation sheet before walking to the second floor and saw that the guests were from the local amusement park, Kings Island. Entering the dining room, I found a group of eight or ten well-fed, but not overly served individuals who seemed to be thoroughly enjoying their evening. After introducing myself, I made some remark about how much the park meant to the area and asked what I could do for them. The head of the party told me this particular group was revamping a train ride through the park, replacing a lot of original buildings with semi-accurate historical structures particular to Warren County. One of the structures was to be the Golden Lamb, as it looked in the early 1800s.

I didn't have the heart to tell them that there were no trains in Lebanon in the early nineteenth century. Instead, my mind was clearly focused on the great exposure we'd get from the thousands of people who would ride the Kings Island train daily. When I asked how they knew what the hotel looked like in the early 1800s, the group leader pulled out a photograph of a painting. The painting, unfortunately, was not of the Golden Lamb but of Ephraim Hathaway's Black Horse Tavern, which was a block north of us. The painting was reproduced in the 1957 book about the Golden Lamb, but as I said, it wasn't our building. I informed the group of the error, but it didn't seem to make much difference. Did I say that the structures were going to be semi-accurate?

Fascinated by the prospect of so much free publicity, I asked if the building was going to be full-size, three quarter-size, half-scale, or what? The group leader informed me that their Golden Lamb was "already done" and that somebody suggested it might be a good idea to "ask" us if they could use our name. "If it's already done…what happens if I say no?" I jokingly asked. He laughed and said they would have just made something up like "The Gray Goose" or "The Red Fox." Who would know the difference? Remember, I said all of this was semi-accurate.

Now, let's get back to architecture. In 1815, the first brick structure comprising the Golden Lamb was a two-story building that is the current lobby and front section of the second floor. Seaman's log tavern stood until 1825, when it was torn down and replaced by the brick building that is now the Lebanon Room and the rest of the second floor. Innkeeper Henry Share built this addition and saw fit to advertise it. In the earliest advertisement ever found for the Golden Lamb, he boasts of "handsome accommodations not excelled by many in the west." Share was so proud of his new addition that he advertised not in the local newspaper, the *Western Star*, but in the *Cincinnati Enquirer*, perhaps in hopes if attracting a wider clientele.

Sometime in the middle to late 1830s, the hotel gained a third floor and began to take on the look that guests recognize today. We know the third floor was added during this period because of a book entitled *Howe's History of Ohio*, published in 1847. In the book is a beautiful engraving with a view that looks north from the base of Broadway Street (by the current train station). The Golden Lamb's three stories are readily evident, along with a couple of chimneys that bit the dust long ago. Stables occupy what is now the area directly outside the gift shop door. A side door facing West Main Street is also visible. The door, which gave quick access to the main part of the building, was walled over on the inside during the early twentieth century. The outside entrance can still be viewed from Gazebo Park; just look for a set of shutters at ground level that don't seem to fit the rest of the building.

The Golden Lamb had three stories until 1874, when the fourth floor was added. The owners, the Stubbs family, probably believed that with the railroads coming to Lebanon, their small town would thrive and grow to become just as big as Cincinnati or Dayton, so more rooms were needed. The railroads came, but the people didn't. Thus Lebanon remained a sleepy little county seat with a much bigger hotel, although gone were the days of "handsome accommodations," as Henry Share promoted his inn.

The old Golden Lamb was certainly "excelled" by many in the west. It had become somewhat down-at-the-heels lodging for monthly boarders and transients. On a postcard from that era, it's bleak, gray, and in need of a good cleaning. It looks like a setting for a gothic horror story.

The hotel would remain unchanged for almost fifty years until 1926, when it was resurrected by Robert Howard Jones. Fresh out of Antioch College and ready to take on the world, Bob Jones purchased the Golden Lamb for the unheard of sum of $6,500. No doubt the locals thought he was crazy to spend that kind of money on such a relic. But Bob thought differently.

He worked as a day assistant manager at the old Van Cleve Hotel, located on the southeast corner of First and Ludlow streets in Dayton, but apparently had very little to do with any of the food service. Claude Cannon, former manager of the Van Cleve, once told me in an interview that Jones was an excellent hotel man, except that he often let his social life and business overlap. Cannon said Jones frequently greeted departing hotel guests in formal attire, not having had time to change from being out the night before. Cannon was sure that the Van Cleve was the only hotel in Dayton that had a desk clerk working in a tuxedo at eight o'clock in the morning.

In an interview before his death, I asked Bob Jones what he remembered about the Golden Lamb in 1926. "There was a bare, 40-watt light bulb hanging in every hotel room," he said, "and cracked plaster everywhere you looked." Jones's grandson, former Second District congressman Rob Portman, remembers his grandfather's tale of taking the mattresses out into the side lot and burning them shortly after he acquired the hotel.

Jones and his partner, Paul Niswonger, dug in their heels and started to bring the aging hotel back to life. With manager Henry Snider, the three began a cleaning and refurbishing program that involved new paint and lighting from the top floor to the bottom. During this period, Jones married a local schoolteacher named Virginia Kunkle. So conscious was he of the propriety of the times, he never entertained his bride-to-be within the walls of the Golden Lamb. Instead, Jones arranged their dates at various eating establishments, lest gossip start about an unmarried woman and her boyfriend who owned the local hotel.

Virginia "Ginny" Jones became Bob's partner not only in life but also in business. She, too, saw a lot of promise in the old hotel that her new husband was slowly bringing back to life. The collections that now reside in the Golden Lamb are the culmination of a lifetime of collecting by Robert and Virginia Jones. Their knowledge and love of antiques and early Ohio furniture and artifacts, along with a keen eye for decorating, eventually made the Golden Lamb a showplace in the Midwest. Note that I said "eventually."

The Golden Lamb was a respectable rooming house and hotel in the late 1920s, but within a few years that would all change. Three years after Jones bought the business, the stock market crashed.

Bob managed to hold onto the hotel and, as he once told me, ". . . even made a little money along the way." The Golden Lamb wasn't flourishing, but it was surviving. Then on December 25, 1932, an event occurred that would foreshadow the future of "Ohio's Oldest Inn." The Lebanon Opera House, located directly across the street from the inn, caught fire.

The opera house had been dedicated on September 2, 1878. At the time, it was termed "The Finest Public Building In Warren County." The three-story gothic structure stood on the northeast corner of Main and Broadway, site of the current Lebanon City Building. With towers on all four corners and a dominating spire in front, the opera house had a 1,200-seat auditorium and was home to everything from high school commencements to programs by the fiery abolitionist, Frederick Douglass, and Henry Ward Beecher, brother of Golden Lamb guest Harriet Beecher Stowe. But by the early 1900s, live theater in America had been supplanted by the big screen, and the old opera house became one more 10-cent theater downtown.

Although arson was suspected in the early morning Christmas Day fire, no charges were ever brought. Flammable reels of film were found throughout the building. Ironically, the movie playing at the time was a little-known and long-forgotten Cary Grant feature called *Hot Saturday*. The old opera house quickly succumbed to the same fate as the previous city building fifty-eight years earlier.

Across the street, Jones had stood on the roof of the Golden Lamb with a hose, ready to douse any errant flames or embers that might jeopardize his hotel. Four years earlier, the fire trucks were on his side of the street, fighting a blaze that threatened to destroy the oldest continuous business in the state of Ohio.

In the early afternoon hours of Monday, April 30, 1928, outdated electrical wiring above the northwest section of the Golden Lamb's fourth floor caught fire and apparently smoldered for some time before being discovered. Fed by unusually high winds at the time, the flames burned through the roof and large sections of the upper story. Jones once told me he had been initially consumed with the cosmetics of the hotel during his previous three years of ownership. So concerned was he with getting rid of the "bare 40-watt light bulbs" and the "cracked plaster" that mechanical upgrades, such as plumbing and electrical, were put on hold while he spruced up the interior and attempted to get customers flowing through the doors once again.

Both Lebanon fire companies responded to the alarm, and by the time they got to the hotel, "black smoke was seen oozing out from under the eaves and through ventilator holes in the roof." Another report stated, "The upper floors were already thick with smoke and it seemed impossible to reach the fire burning between the metal roof and the fourth floor ceiling." The fire companies carried four lines of hose to the fourth floor in an attempt to douse the conflagration.

Realizing the blaze was beyond capabilities of Lebanon's department, the fire chief put out calls to the departments serving nearby Franklin and Mason, who made their runs in record time and provided two additional lines of hose.

By 4:30 in the afternoon, the flames were under control, but the damage was done. A newspaper report stated, "Every room, save a few, at the northeast corner of the building was left dripping in ruins after the fire was extinguished, and the loss from the water is as great as the destruction by fire. Soaking through four floors, plaster fell and the walls were drenched, making it necessary to refinish all but about 10 of the 60 rooms." Showing his spirit, Bob Jones began to re-assemble his hotel in preparation for that night's business as soon as the dripping stopped. Guests that night used what few rooms had not been damaged by fire or water. And before the end of the day, Jones vowed to restore the Golden Lamb, making it bigger and better than ever.

Also damaged in the fire were two businesses that resided on the ground floor of the old hotel. In what is now the Shaker Room, the L.D. Willis Grocery suffered heavy water damage and lost almost all of its merchandise. Next door, in what is now the Buckeye Room, the Famous Auto Supply Company suffered a similar loss, primarily from water leaking through the old plaster ceilings. Though the auto supply store lasted long after the fire, Willis Grocery closed a short time later.

Damage to the building was estimated at $20,000-$25,000. The insurance was split between three local companies headed by Ed. S. Conklin, O.K. Brown and Karl Dakin. Unfortunately, Jones only carried $21,500 of insurance on the building and contents. Undoubtedly he

Kitchen staff 1940s

believed he was amply covered for a building he had paid only $6,500 for just ten years earlier.

As a result of the 1928 fire, the now nationally-known Golden Lamb began to take shape. "After spending our money to rebuild and repair the interior, Virginia and I didn't have enough money to go out and by new furniture, so we went out and bought all of this old stuff," Jones said. He and Ginny went to barn sales, yard sales, and auctions, and purchased what was then second-hand furniture. In the late 1920s, antiques were English or French. The public at large placed little value in good, solid, nineteenth-century American country furniture. It was during the next six years that the Golden Lamb building was sandblasted to restore the original brick, and the now famous two-story colonial balcony was added (a feature that really doesn't belong on a Federal-style structure).

Also during this period, the Joneses started diligently researching the history of the Golden Lamb. With the help of long-time friend and future director of the Warren County Historical Society, Hazel Spencer Phillips, Bob and Ginny began to unearth the rich and colorful legacy of "Ohio's Oldest Inn." The names started appearing on the doors . . . Charles Dickens, Martin Van Buren, Henry Clay, and a host of others.

Other architectural changes came a little more slowly. By the late 1940s, the space formerly occupied by Willis Grocery became a dining room. The northernmost section of the building, now the Buckeye Room, remained an auto parts store and the local AAA office until the late 1950s. By that time, business had increased to the point that Jones reclaimed the space for dining and now had four separate dining rooms on the ground floor. The former auto parts store was christened the Black Horse Room and would remain so until the next major architectural change in 1965.

In mid-1964, Jones unveiled plans for a large expansion to the Golden Lamb with the addition of a two-story structure at the rear of the building, housing an expanded gift shop (located in what is now the Lebanon Room) and a full-service tavern on a lower level for hotel and restaurant guests. Construction began in the fall of 1964 and by the following fall, the old Golden Lamb had been changed once again. The spacious tavern and gift shop addition (built at a cost of $50,000) was completed 162 years after the inn's founding and exactly 150 years from the anniversary of the first brick structure on the property. When the new section opened in 1965, the tavern occupied the lower level while the gift shop was relocated to the site of the current tavern. The Black Horse Tavern featured a six-seat bar, wood-burning fireplace, and enough floor space to accommodate a stage for live entertainment.

Ironically, this marked the first appearance of an actual sit-down bar at the Golden Lamb. Bob Jones had acquired a state license to sell liquor in 1952, but was so worried about offending his long-standing clientele, he kept the license in his desk drawer for five years. Only in 1957 did he begin serving spirits to patrons via a small service bar located in the old Blackhorse Room. Even then (or so I've been told), martinis oftentimes appeared in teacups, and beer bottles were never placed directly on the dining table. In 1971, the locations of the tavern and gift shop were reversed, with the gift shop being moved downstairs to more than double its size. The move also allowed first-floor bar service for restaurant guests.

Not much has changed, externally, since the 1965 addition. Some of the interior walls on the third and fourth floors have been taken out to make larger rooms. Long gone are the public bathrooms on the third and fourth floors, which served travelers for so many years. During a major renovation in the late 1970s, the bathrooms were gutted to expand existing guest rooms. Each bath contained standard commodes, a 1940s-era sink, and a large (very large) porcelain clawfoot bathtub. In the midst of renovations, the tubs (which we thought were worthless) wound up in the dumpster behind the hotel. Only later did we find out that we could have sold the tubs, ten times over, to various guests who all had looks of genuine horror on their faces when they found out what had happened. Who knew?

The next time you see one of those many "historic" depictions of the Golden Lamb, just remember it wasn't always as depicted. And as you see the hotel today, bear in mind that it won't always be this way. The Golden Lamb, like history, is constantly changing and moving forward. What Jonas Seaman established in 1803 bears no resemblance to what Henry Share advertised in 1825. What Bob Jones envisioned in 1926 bears no resemblance to what he created by the end of the 1930s. And the Golden Lamb of today bears no resemblance to what will be twenty or even thirty years from now . . . which is the way it should be. Remaining mindful of its past, and with an eye to the future, "Ohio's Oldest Inn" will remain solid but never stand still.

Charles Dickens, bootleg books . . .
and other furniture-related stories

Are you tired of hearing about Charles Dickens?

I'm not. The author's nasty comments put the Golden Lamb on the map in more ways than one, and I myself can't thank him enough. But in addition to having two rooms named after him, Dickens is honored with two special meals every year, one at Christmas and one in April commemorating the date of his visit. It is this latter celebration that brings us to our first story.

When we hatched the idea of a Dickens celebration in 1981, manager Jack Reynolds began collecting Dickens memorabilia to display in the lobby and throughout the hotel. We already had our Dickens plates and some early etchings and photographs, but Jack felt we needed more. Spying a set of Dickens books for sale in an antique-themed publication, he contacted the seller. The books, the seller explained, were in good condition with not particularly expensive bindings. They weren't rare, he said, but they were complete and the price was right.

The books arrived about a week later, just in time for our Dickens celebration. Jack wanted them solely for display, but I was interested in them for another reason. They were just as the seller described, including an inscription "To Fannie Mae, Christmas 1898." So the books were published prior to 1898.

Here's the wind-up . . .

The antiquity of the books didn't interest me as much as the printing history. After unpacking the volumes, I selected *A Tale of Two Cities* at random and turned to the page bearing the title. I flipped the page and saw only the name of the printer who published the books.

And the pitch . . .

I turned the page, looking for another small inscription, and saw only the familiar words: "It was the best of times, it was the worst of times," the first line of *A Tale of Two Cities.*

HOME RUN!!!!!!

There was NO copyright date. We had purchased, sight unseen and much to my delight, an entire set of bootleg books, and a set for which poor Mr. Dickens didn't receive a dime. I couldn't have been more pleased. As a writer, I'm sorry Dickens got stiffed on his royalties, but lack of a copyright date makes for a great story.

They put the books out every April for the Dickens celebration,

Dickens bootleg books

but if you want to see them and it's not the right time of year, here's
where they are. Walk into the Dickens Room, veer to the left, and look
in the recessed cases near the "in" door to the kitchen. They should be
right there, along with other Dickens memorabilia.

You'll also see a polished copper utensil in one of the cases that
looks like a small shoe with a handle. Its interior is hollow and there
is a spout on one side. Over the years, sharp-eyed customers have
spotted this copper piece and offered a guess as to what exactly it is: an
ale warmer.

Ale was poured into the top, and the flat-bottomed warmer was set
on a stove to heat. Because of the long "foot," the warmer also could be
placed in the coals of a fire if a stove wasn't handy. In either case, the

ale got warm but the handle didn't. Why, though, anyone would want
to drink warm ale is beyond me. Ale was served, for the most part,
warm because refrigeration wasn't exactly commonplace in the 1800s.
But somewhere in the nineteenth century an ingenious coppersmith
fashioned this unique contraption to make the stuff warmer than it
already was. Who knows why.

As long as we're still on the first floor and moving north, there's
something in the Shaker Room that always prompted a lot of
questions, primarily because of its size. If it were smaller, most people
wouldn't notice it. Because of its size, you can't miss it. Hanging on
the west wall, (or dominating the west wall is more like it), is a huge,
pan-shaped creation full of holes. The holes are perfectly round and
very deliberately and evenly spaced. Nobody ventures a guess about
this unique piece anymore, and it's just as well, because its use has long
fallen into obscurity. The Shakers, being big farmers, were also big on
dairies. And what do you get from dairies besides milk and butter? You
get cheese.

The giant cheese press hanging in the Shaker Room probably
produced enough product to keep the Shakers in nachos for a year.
Quite simply, the press was lined with cheesecloth, filled with the
curd, and then a weight was used to press the whey (liquid) from
the mixture. The result was undoubtedly a huge round of cheese,

Ink wells

undoubtedly enough to feed the entire community.

There's a starch strainer, sausage stuffer, and seed stripper in the Shaker Room as well. See if you can find them. I bet you can't.

Let's tell one more story while we're on the first floor. There's a large collection of bottles in the Buckeye Room that had even me fooled for a long time, and probably still mystifies some guests. But once you figure them out, the proverbial light bulb goes off over your head and you simply say, "Oh yeah." On the north wall, near the front of the Buckeye Room, is a clever little shadow box filled with various shapes and sizes of small bottles. They are in numerous shapes and colors, and made of various materials, including glass, bone, and wood. Some are ornate. Some are just plain. They're pretty to look at, and for years I thought that they were just that . . . pretty little bottles.

One day, while helping set up a table directly beneath the collection, I suddenly realized what I had been looking at all those years. These "pretty little bottles" had a singular purpose. Though different people made them at different times and out of different materials, they all served the same purpose. The bottles harken back to a gentler time when a man's signature was important and the ownership of an "inkwell" was a sign of education and importance. Whether these particular inkwells were collected by Robert and Virginia Jones over the years or purchased as a set, they are a clever and significant look back at America's past.

every picture tells a story
the artwork of the Golden Lamb

Mark Twain once said, "Whenever I enjoy something in art that means it must be mighty poor."

The Golden Lamb has acquired a fair collection of paintings over the years, many of them Christmas paintings commissioned between 1970 and 1986, long after the renowned Mr. Twain visited the Lebanon hotel. This Christmas artwork includes oil paintings and watercolors, as well as quilts, samplers, and once, even a hooked rug. Whenever you see a holiday scene at the Golden Lamb, it is undoubtedly one that was done for our annual Christmas card. Unfortunately, we had to suspend the tradition in 1986 when it became cost-prohibitive. Many of the cards, though, are still for sale in our gift shop. Or, if you gush enough over a particular painting, chances are the desk clerk may give you a copy if one's still available. I always did when I worked there.

The selection of an artist for the annual painting was made by hotel manager Jack Reynolds and his wife Sandra. They were always

Cremmins first painting

on the lookout for artists who could provide a unique perspective on "Ohio's Oldest Inn" at Christmas. Many of the paintings are on display throughout the year, and the Golden Lamb attempts to hang most of them during the holidays.

Of all the Christmas scenes, my own personal favorite is a small painting done by then-Cincinnati artist Robert Cremmins for our holiday celebration in 1978. In fact, if there was one thing I could have taken with me when I left in 2001, it would have been Cremmins's painting. The hotel appears much the same as it does today with the full three-story balcony and the restored brick. A truck from the long-forgotten French Bauer Creamery (which was located on West Main Street) carefully navigates a snow-covered street as townspeople gather around a decorated tree in what is now Gazebo Park on the northwest corner of Main and Broadway.

The hotel is the painting's dominant feature, but your eyes are drawn to the small Christmas tree and the people in the park. On the corner is a scene reminiscent of small towns across the country during the holiday season: neighbors gathering together, braving the cold, bundled up against the elements, celebrating Christmas.

In painting this snapshot of small-town life, Cremmins didn't take the easy way out and include coaches and horses and townsfolk in Victorian garb, as had been done so many times before (and after). Instead, with an almost photographic quality and minute attention to detail, the artist captured Lebanon as it undoubtedly was during the period—a small town with honest, caring people who delighted in the simple pleasure of staring at a Christmas tree. The painting didn't have a name, so I was left to my own devices. I immediately titled it, *The Tree In The Town Square*, and had a small nameplate made before anybody could contradict me. It was hung on the south wall in the rear of the Dickens Room, right above what was termed the worst table in the house. If it's not there now, just wander around and look for a small watercolor in an ornate antique frame. It's bound to be around someplace.

Bob Cremmins is the only artist who ever did two Golden Lamb Christmas cards. His second painting was done for our first "Dickens' Of A Christmas" celebration in 1983. He depicted what else . . . the Dickens Room filled with Victorian revelers enjoying a massive holiday feast. Though such a feast undoubtedly never took place, it makes for great artwork. This particular painting usually only gets up during the holidays in one place or another, so you'll have to look to find it.

There is another Dickens painting prominently displayed throughout the year. "Charles Dickens Arriving At The Golden Lamb", 1842, usually hangs behind the desk over the now unused switchboard. It shows a middle-aged, bearded Dickens arriving at the Golden Lamb, standing in front of the familiar red brick structure with its colonial balcony. Townspeople in droves have turned out to meet the famous English author and a crowd has gathered in front of "Ohio's Oldest Inn" to pay him homage. The painting has everything you could want if you like Charles Dickens and the Golden Lamb. The only thing it lacks is any shred of historical accuracy.

In 1842, Dickens didn't look like that, the building didn't look like that, and there certainly wasn't a crowd in town to meet him at the door. If you will remember from a previous chapter, Dickens arrived unannounced, on a public coach, with his wife, her maid . . . Wait a minute. I've told this story once already. Reread the chapter on Dickens if you want the whole thing. His visit went relatively unnoticed in the local press and received only scant mention a couple of days later. As reported in the *Lebanon Star* on Friday April 22, 1842:

> *Mr. Dickens and lady passed through this place on*
> *Wednesday, on their way to Columbus and thence to the Lakes.*
> *Mr. D has been traveling for two weeks past very quietly*
> *in the West, visiting Cincinnati, Louisville, and St. Louis*
> *with intermediate towns; we have been gratified to observe*
> *the total absence of all that parade and sycophancy which*
> *characterized his reception in the Eastern cities. It will give*
> *us a better opinion of ourselves even if Mr. Dickens should not*
> *think the better of us for it.*

There's a fascinating story behind another Christmas painting—a painting you will never see hanging at the Golden Lamb.

Primitive-style artist Tella Kitchen, from Adelphi, Ohio, did a painting for us in the early 1970s that has since been retired to a private collection. Actually, I should say she did two paintings, neither of which is at the Golden Lamb. Intrigued? Read on.

Tella was a 70-something artist when Jack Reynolds first saw her work and asked if she would be interested in doing a painting for our annual Christmas card. At this time, she was "being discovered" by the art world and everybody wanted a piece done by her. Her method of scheduling commissioned works was simple. Solicitors would have to travel to her home in Adelphi for tea and cookies. She told them to pin their business cards to the bulletin board, then said goodbye, wishing them a good day. It was her subtle way of saying, "Don't call me . . . I'll call you."

In 1974, we got the call. Tella visited the inn with her son Denny, viewing previous paintings and Christmas cards. A price was agreed upon and she returned to Adelphi to start work. A month or two went by and she called back.

"Painting's ready!"

The following Sunday, Tella arrived at the Golden Lamb with her finished painting wrapped in brown paper. After breakfast, she set it up in the Dickens Room. It was a great painting, but it wasn't the Golden Lamb, at least not the one most people know. Every artist we commissioned, no matter what time period they were depicting, painted the hotel as it looks today: red brick, four floors, colonial balcony, the whole bit. But Tella, staying true to history, painted a mid-nineteenth century view of the hotel: no balcony, no fourth floor, and

Early Christmas card by Nancy Simpson Bassford

a white paint job over the brick.

Jack stared at her painting for a moment or two. Then the dancing began.

"Tella, it's a marvelous painting," he said, "but . . ." And his voice trailed off.

"It's a great view, and I love the colors, and the local names on the business signs," I said, "but . . ." And my voice trailed off.

We then politely explained that all paintings of the Golden Lamb needed to depict the hotel as it exists today. That's the only Golden Lamb that people recognize. Jack didn't want to lose the artist; he thought Tella Kitchen was destined to prominence. So he took a deep breath and asked, "Do you think you could change it?"

The silence hung in the air for about ten seconds. Then Tella smiled and said, "Let me see what I can do." She wrapped up her painting and went back to Adelphi, and we waited anxiously for a telephone call. After three weeks, we began to wonder if we were ever going to get a call. Then the phone rang.

"Painting's ready!"

Once again, Tella marched in with a canvas wrapped in brown paper. And once again, after breakfast she unwrapped a painting that was to become one of our most popular cards. In three weeks she had done it. Gone was the painted white building, replaced by the warm red brick so familiar to generations of Golden Lamb guests. In place was the fourth floor and the familiar colonial balcony added in the late 1930s. She even added a few of today's downtown buildings that didn't exist in the nineteenth century.

Jack was dumbstruck.

"Tella," he said, "it's perfect." And he added, "I can't believe it's the same painting we saw three weeks ago."

Then Tella dropped the bomb.

"That's because it's not," she confessed with a grin. "I found somebody in Columbus who liked the first one so much, I sold it to them and painted you another one."

So somewhere floating around Columbus is a painting very similar to our 1974 Christmas card. The painting we used hasn't been hung at the Golden Lamb since it went into a private collection in late 1976.

Another unique piece of artwork that's always around somewhere is Will Corson's painting of Gregory Washburn & Co.'s Menagerie (of wild animals) that visited Lebanon in 1872. Look for it hanging over the fireplace in the Lebanon Room just beyond the lobby. If it's not there, ask where it is. It's worth the effort to find it.

For years we had wanted a local circus painting. When nobody offered one, we decided to do our own. At the time, Will Corson was a good friend (he still is) and a primitive-style painter who unfortunately never gained the attention he deserved. After we approached Will with our idea, he began doing some research at the Warren County Historical Society Museum. Laboriously searching microfilm records of century-old *Western Star* newspapers, he found ads for Washburn's Menagerie, promising "an array of animals never before seen in the Midwest" and "free elephant rides for women and children." Tapping his great imagination and abundance of artistic talent, Will captured the menagerie as it paraded down Broadway in front of the Golden Lamb.

The size of Corson's painting is unique. In fact, it's not a painting at all. It's an "overmantle." Two centuries ago during the construction of an expensive home, a blank panel sometimes would be left "over the mantle" for the addition of a piece of artwork. An artist usually would paint a pastoral scene that became a permanent part of the home, just like a window or a wall. Though the Golden Lamb's overmantle isn't permanently attached, it occupies the same spot it would have two centuries ago. (Our overmantle, by the way, is painted on a nineteenth century cabinet door Will found at an auction.)

The story of another holiday painting must be told very carefully because the artist, to the best of my knowledge, is still alive and painting. First, a bit of history. As referenced in a previous chapter, our Christmas celebrations from 1970 to 1993 always had a major theme and a theme ornament. One year our ornament was . . . well, let's just say it was a hat. (It wasn't a hat, but revealing the actual ornament would give away the year and the secret.) When considering artists for that particular year's Christmas card, Jack Reynolds and I both remembered an artist who had exhibited in the Cincinnati Art Club's annual Christmas show at the Golden Lamb. This artist always used hats in paintings—big hats, small hats, all shapes, sizes, colors, and time periods of hats. Sounds crazy, but it worked. The problem was, neither one of us could remember the artist's name. No problem, I said. I would just call up Joe Emmett, who organized the show, and ask him for the artist's name.

Joe said we wanted Mr. Smith. I got the phone number, called the artist and arranged a meeting with Jack and myself. The artist came to the hotel a few days later. I had never seen anyone so excited about doing a Christmas card. We explained the procedure and the theme, agreed upon a price (the most important part), and sat and listened to the artist gush on and on about doing the commission painting.

Jack and I went back to running a busy restaurant and hotel, and the artist rushed home to begin painting the holiday masterpiece. All was well until a couple of weeks later when the artist called and wanted us to view the progress. Jack and I were impressed by the artist's diligence—the painting wasn't due for at least three months—and we were glad to have one less thing to worry about as Christmas approached. The artist came up the next day with an easel and a small light to illuminate the painting from beneath.

With the painting covered up on the easel, our commissioned artist began a speech about how many ideas had come to mind and how many had been rejected before settling upon just the right scene. Then, off came the cover. Wrong artist . . . wrong artist entirely. No multi-colored hats. No hats at all. We found out later we didn't want that Mr. Smith, we wanted another Mr. Smith.

The hats we wanted, the hats we needed to sell the theme, the hats we had waited all summer to see were sadly nowhere to be seen in the painting. What do you do in this situation? If you're a quick thinker like Jack, you say, "It's perfect. Just what we wanted." Whatever happened to the masterpiece? Well, it still hangs every year at the Golden Lamb during the Christmas season, and copies are probably still available in the gift shop. Just don't ask me to tell you which painting it is.

Another year we came up with the great idea of sponsoring a contest to create the Christmas artwork for the Golden Lamb. Quilts happened to be a hot collector's item, so we decided to use quilts, quilt blocks, and quilting materials for decorations. Our holiday tagline was "Christmas Is A Comfort" (comforter . . . quilts . . . get it?) We put the word out that we were looking for original crib-size quilts with a Golden Lamb theme to use for our holiday celebration. The quilt we chose as the most representative would be used for our Christmas card. Also, any other quilts would make a great (and totally free) display for the holiday season.

Jack and I thought maybe we'd get three or four submissions. But sooner than we expected, the quilts started rolling in. First one, then two, then six, then seven and eight. If I remember correctly, we ended up with sixteen of them, all unique in design, color, and execution. Ironically, the first submission was a real stunner and the eventual winner. Cincinnati resident Carolyn Mueller created a small quilt depicting not only the hotel but also a group of quilters working on it, sort of a picture within a picture. This eventually became the standard against which all the others were judged because it was so spectacular. It hangs at the inn during the month of December, but if you come in July and it's not up, ask to see it. It's around somewhere. Jack and I had one regret after that Christmas; we only purchased the winning quilt. There were at least two others we should have bought for our collection.

One of my favorite pieces of artwork depicting the Golden Lamb is one that was never hung on the walls but appeared everywhere else. Sound intriguing? Again, read on.

In the spring of 1987, I was working a Sunday breakfast when I noticed an artist across the street sitting on a bench in front of the city hall. This was not unusual, considering the good view of the inn. Unlike most others, however, this guy was furiously sketching instead of painting. He seemed almost to attack his pad with nothing more than a pencil. He would sketch some, then erase some, and then sketch some more. The artist was there for about an hour and when I looked back again, he was gone. Or so I thought.

Late that afternoon during the break between lunch and dinner, I got a call saying there was someone in the lobby who wanted to see me. Who should be there but my mystery artist. He introduced himself as Bob Bates from Whittier, California. I found out he and his wife Val were also guests of the hotel. Val was an antique dealer, and once a year she and her husband made a swing through the Midwest shopping for merchandise. They funded the trip by selling Bob's sketches. Bob opened up his sketchbook and showed me what he had done in an hour and a half on a Sunday morning sitting on a bench in front of our city hall. In front of me was a glorious 11x17 sketch of the Golden Lamb, complete with the newly constructed gazebo in the park. The sketch was intricate without being mechanical. It was soft but detailed. It was perfect. And it was for sale.

For decades, the standard illustration of the Golden Lamb had been a Caroline Williams drawing that appeared in the *Cincinnati Enquirer* in the 1950s. Bob Jones, the hotel's owner, plastered Williams's illustration on everything from postcards to stationery to menus. We, in turn, had used it on everything from room brochures to coffee cups to t-shirts.

I loved Bob Bates's illustration, though. There was just one big problem. Jack Reynolds always purchased any artwork or antiques for the hotel. The Christmas paintings, Will Corson's overmantle, Lew Hudnall's fireplace screen (I forgot that story . . . maybe in the next book), all had the hotel manager's approval. But on this occasion, Jack was out of town and unreachable, and Bob Bates and his wife were checking out in the morning.

I took a deep breath and asked, "How much?"

Bob smiled. "One hundred and twenty-five dollars and it's yours to use however you please," he replied.

I took another deep breath, walked over to the cash register and made a paid-out slip in the amount of $125, hoping Jack would love Bob Bates's sketch as much as I did and that I hadn't just purchased an illustration of the Golden Lamb for myself.

Three days later, Jack returned to work and approved my expenditure. We replaced the Caroline Williams drawing with Bob's and started putting it on everything. Menus got reprinted, brochures and postcards got the new illustration, and the gift shop had a field day. Jo-Del Clifton, our gift shop buyer, found more uses for that drawing than we could have ever imagined, including plates, Christmas ornaments (three different types), mugs, glasses, calendars, the mandatory t-shirt, sweatshirts, spoons, and a lot more items than I can even remember. It seemed like every time I went out the gift shop door, Jo-Del had yet another souvenir with Bob's illustration on it.

Over the years, Bob and Val Bates became regular guests. Val would haunt the local antique shops and Bob would do sketches to pay for what she bought. He did interior illustrations that we used to promote private dining rooms, and sometime in 2001 or 2002 he colorized the original illustration. I never thought it had the same warmth or simplicity after it was colorized, but that's just me. You can still see the original on the hotel's postcards and printed materials, and the colorized version on numerous souvenirs in the gift shop.

I'm glad I trusted my instincts when I purchased Bob's illustration that Sunday afternoon. If Jack Reynolds hadn't liked it, I'd probably be the owner. That would have been all right, too.

a few words about things
that go bump in the night

Let me begin by saying, I don't believe a word of what
you are about to read. What follows are the made up, wished for,
imagined, concocted and contrived ramblings of guests who perhaps
had one too many martinis in the Black Horse Tavern. They also are
the undocumented, unsubstantiated, believe-it-or-not stories of more
than a few employees who perhaps hyperventilated after walking too
quickly to the fourth floor and saw some strange things while stopping
to rest in front of the Harriet Beecher Stowe Room. As I've already said
. . . I don't believe a word of them. Nevertheless, let me tell you a few
Golden Lamb ghost stories.

People assume that in a building this old and a business even
older, there must be a few spirits floating around the hallways. Well, if
there are, I never saw them, and I spent more time there than anybody.
I've never seen the ghost of Charles Dickens, Mark Twain, Henry Clay,

or anyone else for that matter. I always thought if any guest ever did come back to haunt us, it would be President Warren G. Harding for all the bad things I said about him. But in my thirty-five years at the hotel, I never saw the man. Ghosts do come up at the Golden Lamb, figuratively, but not literally. Stories were told to me over the years about young ghosts, old ghosts, male and female ghosts. Some have reportedly been seen while others have left only supposed traces of their presence. I never bought any of it. I had enough on my mind with the real people populating the place without worrying about the departed.

Certainly we've had our share of deaths under the sign of the Golden Lamb, but as far as I know, and I would know, those people haven't paid any return visits. Eliza Clay, the 12-year-old daughter of Henry Clay, supposedly died at the hotel of what was reported as a "childhood illness" in 1825. Such a tragic death should certainly have sparked a visit or two in over 175 years. Sorry, I haven't seen her. Clement Vallandigham, noted trial lawyer and political activist, who killed himself in his room on the second floor, would be another likely candidate. Punching your own ticket on the eve of the biggest trial of your life is the stuff of O. Henry stories. Mr. Vallandigham was last seen going out the front door in 1872, feet first. And legend has it, he didn't pay his check before he left.

To satisfy guests' cravings for the supernatural, we have to conjure up the names of some lesser-known personages. They're not famous, but that doesn't necessarily mean they can't be ghostly. Our first candidate for supernatural significance is a perfectly innocent young lady named Sarah Stubbs, called "Sally" by her family. The Stubbs family owned the hotel from 1841 until 1914. Sarah's uncle Isaac Stubbs was the tavern keeper while her father, Albert, ran a gristmill just a few miles northeast of Lebanon in Morrow, Ohio. (Today, when you travel from Lebanon to Morrow, you travel on Stubbs Mill Road.)

Albert Stubbs died at an early age and his wife, Eunice, was forced to sell the mill. She came to live under the sign of the Golden Lamb with her young daughter Sarah. Sarah and her mother lived in the family quarters on the second floor of the hotel in an area now occupied by the Presidents Room. Sarah even picked up a few bucks by helping tend the stables, located in the area just outside of the current gift shop door. She grew up, got married, had children and grandchildren, and lived to a ripe old age. Nothing spectacular happened in her life, at least nothing that would make a good ghost story.

Sarah rested peacefully until the mid-1980s when hotel manager Jack Reynolds discovered some furniture that had belonged to her and been used at the Golden Lamb in the nineteenth century. The pieces were in private hands and not in a museum, so Jack had the inspiration to use the furniture to create a child's display room and name it in honor of the late Sarah Stubbs. We had an unused room on the fourth floor that was too small for overnight guests and couldn't be enlarged. Quickly, we arranged for a permanent loan of the furniture and rounded up some kid-friendly period toys and clothes. And faster than you could say "Living History," a new display room was born.

Jack's wife, Sandra, scoured local antique shops to create a room Sarah might have had in the mid-1900s. The two pieces of "original furniture," a nightstand and a rocker, were showcased in the fourth-floor room along with the typical belongings of a nineteenth century child. We made a special point of decorating Sarah's Room for Christmas, Easter, and Valentine's Day, and even moved the furniture around from time to time as if someone actually lived there.

Sarah's Room was originally located in what is now the Harriet Beecher Stowe Room at the head of the stairs on the fourth floor. Bad spot. Guests stopping to view the room caused major traffic congestion for those coming up from the third floor. Plus, having the room by the stairs caused more than one guest to miss the first step as they were looking in the room and not where they were going. It became obvious that Sarah's Room had to be moved.

We found some space directly across the hall in another small storeroom. This room fronted the building and had a great view of

Broadway, although it was considerably smaller than Sarah's former digs across the hall. Well, this was the 1980s, so Sarah would just have to downsize like everybody else. The new room proved to be a great location. Guests saw it as soon as they came up to the fourth floor and it was plenty big enough for a kid who hadn't been around for almost 100 years.

It was shortly after Sarah's move to the front of the building that the stories started. Maids reported hearing strange noises coming from the room early in the mornings as they opened the doors on the unoccupied rooms. Pictures that had been straight in the morning were crooked by afternoon. Toys in the locked room appeared to have been moved. The maids also reported the sounds of stamping feet, as if a child was throwing a tantrum.

Had Sarah returned? Or had she never left? Were these supposed signs Sarah's way of telling us she was sick and tired of being moved from one place to another? Remember, as a child she had lived in Morrow, only to move to the hotel and live on the second floor. In the 1980s, we put her in a room on the fourth floor only to move her again in two years. Was Sarah sick of traveling? Was she tired of wondering from month to month or year to year where she would be living? Was this Sarah Stubbs' way of saying, "ENOUGH! Leave me alone."

Get real, folks. The old hotel building shifts constantly. I stopped trying to figure out all the funny noises in the Golden Lamb decades ago. Whatever anyone thought they saw or thought they heard has a logical and totally rational explanation.

Our second candidate for supernatural stardom, The Honorable Charles R. Sherman, met his death under the sign of the Golden Lamb via perfectly natural circumstances, although rather unexpectedly. Charles Sherman was a revenue collector for Ohio's Third District. Due to the rigors of his profession (collecting taxes from unwilling citizens), it was reported that at age 35 Sherman looked like he was 70. His district covered much of what was then the frontier in Ohio. U.S. bank currency was scarce and most of the revenue was collected with currency backed by local banks. In 1817, Congress passed a resolution stating that the next year only U.S. bank currency would be accepted for any debt to the government. Sherman had six deputies under him who continued to collect the notes issued by local banks. In 1818, when the notes became worthless, he personally took on the debt to the federal government, which he shouldered for the rest of his life.

Sherman was appointed to the Ohio Supreme Court in 1823, and his duties included holding court throughout the territory. He arrived in Lebanon to hold court in June of 1829. After checking into the Golden Lamb (known then as the Ohio and Pennsylvania Hotel), he promptly took ill and died six days later at the age of 40. The esteemed judge was removed from the building, post haste. (Trust me from personal experience. A corpse has a way of killing appetites. But that's a whole other story).

The entire incident would have been a minor footnote in the hotel's history except for reports that the Honorable Judge Sherman still wanders around upstairs in the early hours of the morning and for the fact that Sherman's son Billy became famous. The great general William Tecumseh Sherman, you may remember from your history books, did a little damage and made a name for himself when he marched through Georgia during the latter months of the Civil War. But for those of you unfamiliar with that portion of our nation's history, rent a DVD of *Gone With The Wind* and fast-forward to the last half hour.

As for Justice Sherman, there have been reports over the years (and again I don't believe a word of any of this) of what has been described as a "gaunt gray man" seen in the upstairs hallways. One guest even swears she saw the specter sitting on the edge of her bed when she came back from breakfast one morning. Maids have reported the odor of cigar smoke early in the mornings when they arrived and none of the guest rooms were occupied. Had Justice Sherman returned to Lebanon to gain some peace, having died so suddenly at such a young age so far from home? Maybe he returned to finish trying the cases he left undone in 1829. Maybe his spirit never left and has been wandering the halls for over 175 years. Maybe he just forgot his umbrella.

Give it a rest. There are no ghosts in the building.

Our final alleged ghost may or may not have died in the Golden Lamb. (I say she did.) John Zimkus, my long-time friend and local historian, claims she died elsewhere. If John wants to promote his case, let him write his own book. (It would be a bestseller.)

Eliza Clay, youngest daughter of famed legislator Henry Clay, often traveled with her father back and forth from their home in Kentucky to Washington D.C. In July of 1825, 12-year-old Eliza, her father, and her mother, Lucretia, were making a trip to Washington and of course stopped in Lebanon on the way. Eliza, who developed a fever in Cincinnati, was treated by a local physician for what was reported to be a "childhood illness." Her condition was considered "serious but not life threatening."

Assured that Eliza would recover, Henry Clay left Lebanon on August 11, 1829, for the arduous trip across the mountains to Washington D.C. He arrived in the capital city ten days later, only to read in the *National Intelligencer* that his daughter had died shortly after his departure from Lebanon. Eliza Clay was buried in Pioneer Cemetery on Main Street for a number of years until the body was exhumed and moved to the family plot in Kentucky. Flowers were placed at the empty gravesite for a number of years as well.

Golden Lamb guests have reported hearing the giggling of a young girl in the hallways late in the evening as they toured the hotel's rooms. One guest swore she felt someone or something stroking the hem of her mink coat, much like you would stroke a cat. Glancing down, she saw a young girl, dressed in nineteenth century bedclothes, who then ran down the hallway and around the corner. Other guests have reported seeing the face of a young girl peeking around the corners of the hallways on the third floor.

Then there's me, who worked at the Golden Lamb for ten hours a day, six days a week, for thirty-five years, and never saw anything or anybody.

You decide whom to believe.

Corwin Room

one room...one day...

that's all we want! Movies and television at The Golden Lamb

Anytime someone called and wanted to bring a film crew to the hotel, I cringed. Filming inside the building during normal hours, whether for television or movies, and even taking still photographs, disrupted our routine and seemed to disturb and fascinate the guests at the same time. Cables were snaked all over the floors, lights brought in were constantly blowing our circuit breakers, and the crews inevitably wanted free lunch.

Filming was a double-edged sword. On one hand, we couldn't buy that kind of publicity and exposure on television or in a magazine article. On the other hand, we had to put up with a group of strangers who felt they had free rein to go anywhere and take as long as they liked to do their job. Never mind that we had guests to serve, rooms to rent, and a business to run.

I learned, early-on, if a television crew said they were going to be at the hotel "around" 11 in the morning, that meant maybe by 2 in the afternoon. And if a shot was going to take "just a few minutes," figure on at least half an hour. And the fewer people, the better. Whenever shooting involved more people than the on-air personality and a camera person, I knew to cancel any plans I had for dinner.

We were always a popular stop for local TV stations, especially around the holidays when, ironically, we didn't need the exposure. We herded more than a thousand people a day through the restaurant during the Christmas season, thank you very much, with no advertising and no publicity. Nevertheless, we kept hoping that the crew we bent over backwards for in December would remember us in March, when we really needed the exposure. Unfortunately, it never happened.

Two feature films have been shot in Lebanon: *Harper Valley PTA*, a low-budget movie made in 1981; and *Milk Money*, a big-budget production shot in the early '90s. Each brought a few weeks of glitz and glamour to town. The Golden Lamb had very little to do with *Harper Valley PTA*, but we got involved in a big way with *Milk Money*, and therein lies a tale.

Harper Valley PTA was a local production by Phil Borack, a theater operator and filmmaker from Cincinnati. The movie was based on the '60s hit song by the same name (whatever happened to Jeannie C. Riley?) and as one story goes, Borack took out a compass and drew a forty-mile radius around Cincinnati, searching for the perfect location to shoot his small-town story. Guess what small southwestern Ohio town was within the circle? Borack, who once managed the long-forgotten Old Fort Drive-In Theater in Lebanon, remembered the town and its quaint atmosphere. Because we were close and we fit the profile, voila! Lebanon became Harper Valley for about two weeks.

Featured in the film are the old Lebanon Middle School on North Broadway, the Village Ice Cream Parlor, a private home on Deerfield Road, Jerry Miller's home on Cincinnati Avenue, and the beautiful Ulrich farm on West State Route 63. As for the Golden Lamb's involvement, a few of the cast stopped in the hotel for dinner, most notably Barbara Eden (remember the '60s sitcom *I Dream of Jeannie?*) and her co-star, Ronnie Cox. I missed them both. My only brush with fame came when I got Kleenex for Nanette Fabray.

The movie was released decades ago, but visitors still ask about it. They want to visit the ice cream parlor and see the house on Deerfield Road where Barbara Eden's character, Stella Johnson, lived. For a film that had a short shelf-life and went straight to the drive-ins, *Harper Valley PTA* still has an almost cult-like following.

Milk Money starred Melanie Griffith and Ed Harris, and was directed by well-known actor and director Richard Benjamin. How they wound up in Lebanon, I have no idea. As I said, this was a big-budget project; the producers weren't looking to cut corners like the *Harper Valley PTA* folks.

I spotted Richard Benjamin in the hotel twice before news of the movie broke. I didn't think much about seeing him because a lot of media people who were in Cincinnati found their way to Lebanon for a day or two to check out antique shops and enjoy life in the "country." Several weeks later, however, the *Western Star* breathlessly reported on its front page that a Hollywood film crew was coming to town and Lebanon would be turned into Middletown, Pennsylvania, for the duration of their stay. The plot, I think, was about a young boy who sets out to find a wife for his widowed father, played by Ed Harris. I think the candidate, Ms. Griffith, had a less-than-perfect past, which helped propel the movie and supposedly made it funny.

I wrote, "I think," twice in the above paragraph for a very good reason. Even though *Milk Money* was released in 1994 and apparently is still shown occasionally on cable TV, I have never seen the movie. Why would I avoid watching a major motion picture that has the Golden Lamb and Lebanon in it? Read on.

Shortly after the formal announcement, I came to work one afternoon and was promptly informed that someone was waiting for me in the Black Horse Tavern. Walking into the bar, I immediately saw someone who had to be with "the movie," a term that would be on everyone's lips for the next two weeks. If someone wanted to block off the street, it was because of "the movie." If a business was asked to close early, it was because of "the movie." If someone, anyone, wanted to double-park in the street, it was because of "the movie." I was waiting for someone to come in and ask for free dinner and drinks because they were associated with "the movie." It never happened, but that's about the only thing they didn't ask for.

The person waiting for me was definitely associated with "the movie." Sitting on a barstool and talking on a cell phone (one of the first I had ever seen), the gentleman wore faded blue jeans and a blue work shirt that was somewhat unbuttoned and exposing lots of gold jewelry. He also had on cowboy boots. His hair was sun-bleached, his tan un-natural, and his sunglasses pushed back on his head. The guy was a walking billboard for every California cliché ever written. He was also, I found out later, drinking anisette from a bottle that had been on the shelf for about three years. We weren't a big anisette type of place.

I politely stood in the doorway until he had completed his call and then walked forward and extended my hand.

"Hello," I said. "My name is Fred Compton . . . I understand you want to see me."

CUT!

We're going to stop here for just a moment. Don't worry . . . we'll come back. Remember, I'm in the tavern and I just introduced myself to someone from "the movie."

We're stopping because I want to ask that the next time you watch a movie, watch it all the way to the end. I don't mean to the point where it says THE END on the screen. I mean all the way until there's nothing left to watch.

As the credits roll down the screen, you will see the hundreds of people needed to make a movie. Most of the names, and many of the terms, will be unfamiliar. For example, there will be someone called a "gaffer." A gaffer is a person hired as an electrician. That's all he does. Also listed will be a "best boy." The best boy (who could be a girl) is the electrician's assistant. That's all he or she does. Somewhere on the list will be the "Foley Editor," whose job it is to insert sound effects into the movie, such as gunshots and squeaking doors. That's all this person does.

High up on the credit list will be the "Location Director." The location director is the person hired to lie to people. That's all he does.

AND . . . ACTION!

"Hey Fred, how are you?" the man said, extending his hand but still glued to his barstool. "My name is Nathan and I'm the location director for the production *Milk Money*, starring Ed Harris, Melanie Griffith, and directed by Richard Benjamin."

Let the lying begin!

"You know Fred—can I call you Fred?—I've been in town for a couple of days and all I hear about is the Golden Lamb. Fred, even in California where I live, people know about this place. The Golden Lamb has such a prestigious reputation with all of your history and all the presidents and authors who have stayed here. There aren't many businesses that have the prestige of being almost 200 years old and still operating. The building, the furnishings, all of these antiques, Fred, are just unbelievable. I've got collector friends in California who would drool, I mean really drool, over most of this stuff. It must have taken a lot of years to build up such a prestigious collection."

I had heard this same speech hundreds of times during my, at that point, twenty-some years of innkeeping. Whenever the person got to the third "prestigious," my inclination was to grab my wallet and say, "Just cut the crap. What do you want? What . . . Do . . . You . . . Want?"

This speech, no matter who gave it, was always followed by a plea for dinner-for-two as a fundraiser prize, advertising on a phone

Formal Dining Room — now The Lebanon Room

book cover or in a horse show program, or a free meeting room for an organization. They always wanted something.

Nathan wanted to film a scene for the movie in the hotel. Having been through extended filming a couple of times before, I had a much-practiced, diplomatic answer ready for my new best friend.

NO!

Nathan kept repeating, "Fred, we just need one room for one day. That's all we want."

NO!

"But Fred . . . think of the publicity. One room . . . one day . . . that's all we want. This is a major motion picture . . . seen all over the world. Wouldn't you like the Golden Lamb to be seen all over the world?"

NO!

Now he was begging.

"Fred," he pleaded. "One room . . . one day. I promise."

Against my better judgment, I caved. Jack Reynolds, Nathan and I agreed on a shooting schedule and a location. We would let them film in the Dickens Room after 6:30 in the evening, for one night only. Jack even managed to rent a few rooms to the production company as a bonus.

I forgot about the filming until a few weeks later when I came to work and saw that the city parking lot had been taken over by "the movie." Later that afternoon, I was having lunch with Jack when we saw a curious figure enter the dining room and walk straight toward us. He was a young guy with the shoulders of a linebacker and the arms of a weightlifter. He was wearing cut-off blue jean shorts, work boots and a skin-tight T-shirt that said in big letters, "KOJACK... Production Staff." Around his waist was a tool belt . . . fully loaded.

As this guy got to our table, he thrust out his hand and said, "Hi. My name is Tim. I'm the lead set coordinator for the movie *Milk Money.*"

Then he dropped the bomb.

"I've been in town a couple of days," he said, smiling all the while, "and I've found it's easiest to do it this way. You tell me what Nathan told you, and then I'm going to tell you the truth."

Of course the truth bore no resemblance to the now-familiar refrain, "one room . . . one day."

According to Tim, filming was to take place in the Lebanon Room, not the Dickens Room, and the crew would need the room for the entire night—unless they needed it for two nights . . . certainly no more than three!

No, Tim. Wrong room. Wrong time.

"Uh . . . Nathan mentioned something about you feeding the extras dinner," said Tim.

"Uh . . . only if they pay," I replied.

"Uh . . . Nathan did tell you about the lights?" Tim asked with a grin on his face.

"Uh . . . yes. He mentioned there would be a 1,000-watt light for the scene," I said, steeling myself for the response.

"Uh . . . the lights are 1,000 watts, but we'll have eight of them in the room."

When Tim said eight lights, I just about fainted. I envisioned Warren County's largest tanning booth in the Dickens Room. But I had an easy way out, or so I thought. I told him our system couldn't possibly handle 8,000 watts.

"Oh, not to worry, Fred," Tim said. "The lights run off of a generator."

What generator?

"The generator we just unloaded in your parking lot. Don't worry . . . it only takes up about five parking spaces. Should be gone in about a week."

By late afternoon, there were cables snaked from the parking lot, through the basement, up the stairs, and through the lobby into the Dickens Room. I immediately went looking for Tim.

"Those cables on the floor have got to go," I said, "They're a lawsuit waiting to happen."

"Don't worry, Fred," said Tim, putting a beefy arm around my shoulders. "Come back in half an hour. You won't even know they're here. We're in the movie business, Fred. We make . . . magic."

With reassurance like that, who was I to worry? I came back in half an hour to find Tim's "magic" consisted of securing the cables to the carpet with duct tape. The "magic," I guess, was that he used red duct tape to match the carpet.

For the movie, Lebanon, Ohio, would be turned into Middletown, Pennsylvania. Every vestige of "Lebanon" and "Ohio" had to be obliterated from shops, street signs, and the like. For us, the movie company had large pieces of magnetized rubber painted to exactly match our sign, which covered up the words "Ohio's Oldest Inn." When I saw the guy in the bucket crane covering up both sides of the sign, I had to admit I was impressed with the thoroughness. Chances are the sign would never be seen, and even if it were, would the audience be able to pick out those three words?

Looking up the street, I saw another crane in front of Lebanon Citizens National Bank, where workers positioned a 10-by-12-foot replication of the bank's façade, thereby turning it into Middletown Citizens National Bank. The replication had a faux marble background and gold lettering just like the original. Once in place, it looked like it had been there forever. Then it hit me. Lebanon Citizens got a whole new front for their building while the "prestigious" Golden Lamb got two giant refrigerator magnets.

The filming proceeded for about ten days with more than a little disruption. Streets were blocked off, crews filmed late into the night, stores had to close early, and there was absolutely no place to park downtown. I never saw Melanie Griffith or Ed Harris, and I sure never saw the infamous Nathan, who started the whole thing. I did see director Richard Benjamin a couple of times, sitting in his director's chair and shouting, "Action!" (Yeah, directors really do that.) My brief brush with fame this time was selling a jar of celery seed dressing to Melanie Griffith's mother, the actress Tippi Hedren . . .

Two national television crews came to the Golden Lamb in 1997 and, for the most part, they behaved themselves. TV crews had fewer members, they didn't stick around as long as film crews, plus they didn't drag 8,000 watts of light around with them, so they were usually easier to work with and accommodate. I said "usually." The exception were crews that filmed TV commercials. Yeah, we had a few of those, too. Every commercial producer thought he (or she) was the next Spielberg or Fellini and their ad for bed linens or furniture polish was going to propel them into the big-time.

One producer, filming a commercial in the Dickens

Vallandigham Room

Bedroom, made some poor model pull down a bedspread nineteen times before he was satisfied he had "got his shot." Another required a clean rag for each of the twenty-two times his model wiped an imaginary spot off of a table in the Vallandigham Room to hawk furniture polish. By the end of that filming, the table had to be the cleanest piece of furniture in the hotel. And no doubt the model's hand smelled lemony fresh for several months to come.

But for the most part, the attitude of the TV crews was, "Get in, get the shot, go home."

Early in 1997, I took a call from a young producer from C-Span, the cable channel that televises live sessions of Congress and that, as far as I can tell, nobody ever watches. The producer told me they wanted to film at an authentic country inn. When I remarked to the young man that I thought all C-Span did was aim a camera at the floor of the Senate and walk away, he informed me that besides feeding the egos of obscure congressman and senators (my words, not his), C-Span also produced news and literary programs.

A C-Span crew was retracing the steps of Alexis de Tocqueville. For those of you not up on your nineteenth century French authors (and you know who you are!), de Tocqueville was a latter-day Charles Kuralt who rode around the United States and wrote about what he saw. After listening to a rather lengthy explanation of the project, I told the producer that I was familiar with de Tocqueville and his writings. I also informed him that I had never heard de Tocqueville's name mentioned in connection with southwestern Ohio, let alone the Golden Lamb. In other words, if the writer had been here, I'd know about it.

The producer sheepishly admitted, "Well, in all honesty, the closest he ever got to you was Cleveland. And we couldn't find a decent country inn around Cleveland, so we're coming down to see you."

Several weeks later, C-Span filmed a carefully worded and edited six-minute segment. Never once did we say de Tocqueville was ever actually at the Golden Lamb. But it sure sounded like he was. On camera, I was lobbed softball questions such as, "In de Tocqueville's time, what was a typical meal at the Golden Lamb?" Or, "In de

Tocqueville's era, how much of the building was here and what did it look like?" By the end of the interview, I had danced around the truth so much, my legs were tired. But with editing and lots of dramatic shots of furniture, the piece was totally believable on television several weeks later. My six minutes aired at 6:55 a.m., sandwiched between segments on unrest in the Middle East and high oil prices. Come to think of it, they could probably run the same three stories today and nobody would know the difference.

A few weeks later, I got a call from the fledgling Home and Garden Television network. HGTV wanted to film a story on our Shaker collection for a program cleverly titled, *The Furniture Show*. The producer, Phil Watson, had gotten our name from Dave Smith of The Workshops of David T. Smith in Morrow. (The only two reproduction antiques in the Golden Lamb were made by Dave Smith. They've sat in the same spot for over twenty- five years and nobody has ever questioned their pedigree or authenticity. For enough money, I'll tell you where they are.)

During our initial conversation, Watson asked me if I could line up a Shaker expert to do the on-camera interview and commentary. At that time, the only Shaker expert I knew was our good friend Chuck Muller, editor and publisher of the *Antique Review*, and somehow I just couldn't ask Chuck to drive down from northern Ohio and be here at

8:30 in the morning for fifteen minutes of filming . . . for free.

So once again I became the resident expert, this time on Shaker. I wasn't then, nor am I now, an expert on Shaker, but I knew enough to fake it and sound convincing. Again, with careful editing and dramatic shots, the piece played well on the cable channel—again and again and again. It played about two dozen times over the next two years and brought us lots of exposure. Phil Watson and his one-person crew (remember, the smaller the better) were in and out with little or no disruption to the Golden Lamb or its guests.

Undoubtedly the best piece of television ever done on the hotel was filmed in 1975. It was four minutes of pure gold (excuse the pun) that aired one time only that year and then not again until almost two decades later. It was worth the wait.

The story began on a busy Monday afternoon at the height of lunch when I answered the telephone. At that time, we were still using the switchboard, which required plugging in a cord and throwing a switch to answer a call. The board buzzed, I plugged in a cord, threw the switch and quickly gave my normal greeting during the lunch rush.

"GoodafternoontheGoldenLamb . . . MayIhelpyouplease."

And then I heard the voice. A voice I had heard on radio. A voice I had heard on television. A voice that belonged to the author of books I had read over and over again because the writing was so beautiful. And the voice said, "This is Charles Kuralt. To whom am I speaking?"

Now at this time, I was just eighteen months removed from college with a journalism degree, and here I was talking to one of the foremost media personalities of the day. I was so nervous I threw the wrong key on the old switchboard and hung up on the legendary CBS correspondent. Ten seconds later, the phone buzzed again and the voice repeated, "This is Charles Kuralt. To whom am I speaking? And PLEASE don't hang up."

In talking with Kuralt, I discovered he was on assignment from CBS News, compiling a program called, "On The Road To '76". It was his job to find the most historic spot in each of the fifty states and do a four-minute segment for the *Evening News with Walter Cronkite*. Kuralt was in Chillicothe, preparing to film his Ohio segment on the Battle of Fallen Timbers, the major Indian battle that opened up the Northwest Territory for settlement. In Chillicothe, someone told him about Lebanon. "Got an old hotel over there," the person said. "Place called the Golden Lamb."

Kuralt and his crew of three drove over to Lebanon in the now famous motor home to look at our "old hotel." After Jack and I escorted him around town for a couple of hours, Kuralt forgot all about Chillicothe. He had found what he thought was the most historic spot in the state of Ohio.

The CBS crew filmed for three days, and we were impressed by the fact that they didn't ask for a thing. We offered complimentary rooms, free meals, anything to show our appreciation. They refused. As Kuralt explained, "CBS News may hang me from a high tree when they find out I filmed this in a commercial establishment. But this place is worth it. I had better be able to show complete expenses for this one."

Our segment didn't air until December of 1975, and as with every December we barely had time to watch. At 6:50 on a Friday night, we gathered around the television set in the Black Horse Tavern and watched ourselves on the *CBS Evening News*. Four minutes later, we went back to work and it was business as usual.

We tried in vain to get a copy of the program. Any copy that CBS News might provide, however, would have been on professional-size videotape and we didn't have the capability of playing it. This was 1975, before there were VCRs in everyone's home. We kept looking for a copy, but by the end of 1976 we had more or less forgotten about it.

Fast-forward almost twenty years. Late in the summer of 1994, our sous chef, Dennis Glosser, stopped me in the kitchen and said, "My father was watching Charles Kuralt on the Travel Channel and he did a story on the Golden Lamb."

The first words out of my mouth were, "Dennis . . . please . . . please tell me he taped it."

Dennis said, "Yeah, I think he did."

The next day Dennis came in with a VHS tape with four minutes of video none of us had seen in almost twenty years. We gathered around a TV in the Presidents Room, popped in the tape, and it was 1975 all over again. There was the opening shot of the Regina music box playing "Home Sweet Home" while Charles Kuralt did a voiceover about the Golden Lamb. He talked about the long-forgotten canal system in Lebanon, early transportation, and a few of our famous guests. The photography was beautiful, and Kuralt's voice was as melodic as ever. In watching the Black Horse Tavern segment, I saw guests who today were a little grayer, a little heavier, and unfortunately a few who weren't around anymore.

There came a point in the tape I had totally forgotten. Kuralt is sitting in one of our big wingback chairs by the fireplace, holding a reproduction copy of a nineteenth century *Western Star* newspaper we found somewhere. As the camera slowly zooms in, he puts down the newspaper and says, "If a man could have only lived long enough, he could have sat in the lobby of the old Golden Lamb Hotel and watched the entire history of a nation pass by."

I don't really know why, but standing in the dining room that day, between shifts, watching that tape, and after almost thirty years of walking in the same front door every day, it suddenly hit me. At that time, the Golden Lamb had been sitting quietly on the corner for over 190 years, watching the world change in ways no one could have ever imagined. When the War of 1812 began, the Golden Lamb had been in business for nine years. When the Civil War was being waged several states away, we had been in business for well over half a century. When the "war to end all wars" was being fought half a world away, we already had celebrated our 100th birthday. The immensity of it was somewhat overwhelming. Business had come and gone, presidents and heads of state had changed innumerable times, boundaries had changed, even names of countries, but we were still there.

Guests of the Golden Lamb started out traveling on foot, then graduated to horses and wagons, and later took advantage of the new-fangled canals and railroads. They stood on our balcony and watched Lem Kilpatrick, who owned Lebanon's first automobile, come chugging up Broadway. They no doubt laughed and swore it would never last, but last it did. From horse-drawn wagons to an age when a man went to the moon and back, we were there.

the quilt that wouldn't die
and other furniture related stories

Deceptive advertising and dirty politics are nothing new. There's a humdinger of an example on our second floor, which is as good a place as any to start this installment of furniture tales. Pull on your hiking boots because we're going to cover three stories and about a hundred years of American history in the next few pages.

At the end of the north hallway, on the second floor of the hotel, is a dining room named for Lebanon resident Thomas Corwin. Corwin was a hometown boy who made good in the nineteenth century. Born in Kentucky, he was 4 years old when his family moved to Lebanon. Corwin had a distinguished political career that included stints as the Warren County prosecuting attorney, the governor of Ohio, the 20th secretary of the U.S. Treasury, and ambassador to Mexico. Somewhere along the way, he also became the 12th president of the United States. Confused? Read on.

Nicknamed "The Wagon Boy," Corwin mounted a less-than-stellar campaign against the eventual 12th U.S. president, Zachary Taylor. Part of Corwin's campaign was a small political advertisement with his portrait. Underneath are the words:

Thomas Corwin

12th President of The United States

The Golden Lamb has one of these ads framed somewhere on the second floor. You will have to look for it because it tends to move around. Guests see it and begin wondering. Time and time again, I have seen people mentally reconstructing presidential succession in their heads, trying to figure out where Corwin fits in. Well, we know he doesn't fit in. Guests who closely examine the declaration under the portrait will see:

Thomas Corwin

The People's Choice For

12th President of The United States

The middle line, of course, is set in much smaller type than the top and bottom lines, proving political misdirection was not invented in the twentieth century.

There is another small piece (this one moves around, too) in the Corwin Room, which, in my opinion, is one of the Golden Lamb's most unique artifacts: a set of five calling cards that belonged to Thomas Corwin. As an antique, the set probably isn't worth much. It certainly isn't very impressive to look at. But today, when virtually everyone has a business card of some type, Corwin's calling cards are nineteenth century mementos that signify rank and honor.

The first card says, "Thomas Corwin, Ohio," signifying the beginning of his political career as governor. The second card reads, "Thomas Corwin, Secretary of the Treasury." Corwin has now moved up the political ladder to cabinet rank. The third card states in true nineteenth century hyperbole, "Thomas Corwin, Envoy Extraordinary and Minister Plenipotentiary of The United States." Our "Wagon Boy" has reached the zenith of his career as ambassador to Mexico. The final two cards read simply, "Mr. and Mrs. Thomas Corwin, At Home." Corwin has retired and is accepting visitors who might be inclined to call.

Walking back down the hallway on the second floor and glancing into the Presidents Room, you'll see another set of "paired portraits" similar to the ones hanging downstairs. I have no idea who these people are. On the insurance inventory, they are simply listed as "portrait unknown man" and "portrait unknown woman."

At the end of the hallway, just outside the ladies room, is an interesting set of Royal Doulton china with Dickens characters and scenes. Golden Lamb owners Robert and Virginia Jones made a lengthy trip to England and Scotland in 1959, picking up lots of antiques along the way. This set of dishes and the case were among their finds. The plates went relatively unnoticed until the early 1980s when we started our annual Dickens celebration. The first year, gathering up all the Dickens memorabilia he could find, hotel manager Jack Reynolds moved the entire case to the lobby for display during the two-week celebration. Regular guests, who no doubt had passed right by the plates numerous times, noticed the spectacular "new collection" and asked where we got them. "Found 'em by the bathroom," was my standard reply.

The Dickens bedroom is also on the second floor. Room 36 is undoubtedly the most requested overnight room at the Golden Lamb. With its ornately carved Victorian headboard and matching

Dickens bed

168

mirror, it's a favorite for honeymoon couples and those Anglophiles wanting the true Dickens experience. I wouldn't sleep there if you paid me. Well, maybe if you paid me. It's a perfectly nice room. The bed's comfortable, the plumbing works, and it's close to the lobby. But as regular guests know, the hotel tends to get busy. Occupants of the Dickens bedroom, unfortunately, must put up with all the foot traffic in the second floor hallway leading to the private dining rooms. And honeymooners, be forewarned. You might want to keep the shades down, as this room also has two windows that look out on the second-floor balcony.

For my money, give me Room 30 at the rear of the second floor, or Room 20 on the third floor, or any of the big doubles on the fourth floor. The higher up the room, the less traffic and noise you have to put up with. And speaking of Room 30, let's take a short walk down the hall and I'll tell you an interesting, totally non-historical story about a piece of furniture I've nicknamed, "Our Killer Bed."

Room 30 originally was named for President William McKinley. Unfortunately, McKinley got bumped in 2004 when President George W. Bush came to town. It was only appropriate, given the fact that Bush's mother, Barbara, stayed in this room when she was campaigning for Bush's father in 1988. Naming a room after a living person broke the long-standing rule, but hey, it wasn't my decision.

In the George Bush Room is a very large four-poster plantation bed with a very unique flat canopy. Rather than being arched like most canopies, this one is framed in the same mahogany as the bedposts and is covered from corner to corner with fabric that features a large, gathered, fabric rosette in the middle. Now remember that description: dark mahogany all around, flat fabric frame, rosette in the middle.

I ran across a file many years ago that explained how this particular bed came to rest under the sign of the Golden Lamb. It had been transported by flatboat from Mississippi to New Orleans and resided in the home of a wealthy industrialist for almost sixty years before making its way somehow to Cincinnati. In the late 1950s, the owners decided to give the bed to Robert and Virginia Jones on the condition that it be used in one of the Golden Lamb's overnight guest rooms and always be on public display. It was originally put in Room 2 on the fourth floor and was part of the Taft Suite. (In the 1980s, we divided these rooms, but that's another architecture story, maybe for volume two.)

As the story was told to me, a salesman was staying at the inn during the early 1960s. His name is neither remembered nor important for our purposes. After lifting probably a few too many glasses, he eventually made his way to his room on the fourth floor and collapsed in the canopied bed, fully clothed. The next morning when the salesman checked out, he appeared a little shaken and nervous. When questioned by our desk clerk, Martha Beel (there's a person who deserves her own chapter), he said he awoke fully dressed, with his shoes on, and found himself staring up at that huge silk rosette framed in gleaming mahogany. For a brief, terrifying moment, he thought he had died and was lying in a casket! If you ever have occasion to lie in that bed, try it. You'll see what the traveling salesman meant.

The killer bed

Let's skip to the fourth floor and I'll tell you a story about a popular artifact I dubbed, "The Quilt That Wouldn't Die." How we got the quilt is an interesting but fairly mundane story. How it ended up on the fourth floor is a whole other matter.

In early 1975, Jack Reynolds decided to make a major acquisition for the hotel in honor of the nation's bicentennial celebration. And why not? If anyone could take advantage of the patriotic fervor about to sweep the country, and milk it for all it was worth, it was us. Jack commissioned nationally known quilter and artist Mary Borkowski, of Dayton, to design and create a full-size quilt with a patriotic theme. It would hang at the Golden Lamb throughout the bicentennial.

Jack had a "few" things he wanted on the quilt. He wanted to make sure there was a reference to the bicentennial, the state of Ohio, the state bird, the state flower, the Golden Lamb, stagecoach travel, and of course don't forget the ten dead presidents. I began envisioning a quilt large enough to cover an entire wall and then some. Mary merely took Jack's list, went back to Dayton, and started sewing.

We received some rough sketches in the coming months as ideas went back and forth. But for the most part, Mary was more than a little secretive about the final design. She delivered the quilt in December, (right at the height of Christmas), and it was everything we had anticipated and more. Mary incorporated all of Jack's ideas and more than a few of her own, creating a massive work of art that not only celebrated the nation's bicentennial, but the Golden Lamb and the State of Ohio as well. In addition to Jack's suggestions, she also included an outline of each of the fifty states and the ten presidential signatures.

We had a frame constructed, put the quilt behind plexiglass, and displayed it in the lobby beginning in May, 1976. We had a lot going on that year, including a totally new dining room menu and an ambitious fourteen-week series of meals titled, "A Taste of America… Our Heritage in Food". In addition, it seemed like we had a TV crew in the hotel every other day filming a warm and fuzzy patriotic spot for the local news.

In February, 1977, when the dust had settled from both Christmas and the bicentennial, we took the quilt down, stored it in the fourth-floor storeroom, and began planning our next promotion. Then the phone calls started.

"What happened to the quilt?"

"Was the quilt stolen?"

"Did the owner take the quilt back?"

And my own personal favorite: "I heard the quilt was raffled off for charity. Why wasn't it published in the newspaper?"

The calls continued until Jack and I almost simultaneously said, "Enough!!!" We cleared some space on a wall on the second floor, re-hung the quilt, then went back to running our restaurant. The piece proved just as popular with guests, even after the bicentennial. It was the subject of several newspaper stories, photographed for an article on patriotic art, and even loaned out a couple of times to museums for display.

In 1982, the upstairs hallway needed new wallpaper and the quilt had to come down in order to finish the job. Once again it was carefully packed away on the fourth floor. After the wallpaper was put up, we replaced the quilt with a collection of Currier & Ives prints that had been gathering dust in an upstairs room. And once again, we went back to running our restaurant.

Of course it didn't take long. The phone started ringing, with callers asking the same questions.

"What happened to the quilt?"

"Was the quilt stolen?"

"Did you sell the quilt?"

This time, Jack and I didn't fool around. A space was quickly cleared in the fourth floor hallway for the quilt, where it remains to this day. We loaned it out again a couple of times over the years, but always with a note in the empty frame stating that no, it hadn't been stolen. No, we didn't sell it. And no, the owner didn't come and take it back. For what was to be a short-lived display, the quilt took on a life of its own. Another hundred years or so and it will be in the same must-see category as the Regina music box, the Dickens bed, and the lamb with the bullet holes in it.

A lamb with bullet holes, you say? That's a whole other chapter.

history found and
history lost forever.
The mystery of the Marilyn.

The mystery began with the death of Lebanon resident Scott McClure, who passed away in 1988 at the age of 94. Scott was the only person I ever met who actually knew Shakers. Their holdings abutted his family farm, and in his later years Scott told me stories about his neighbors, such as their habit of taking in every stray animal that wandered by.

Scott McClure left a farmhouse crammed with almost a century's worth of papers and memorabilia. When his heirs cleaned out the place, they found an item relating to the Golden Lamb and graciously passed it along to me. It was a colorful three-section cardboard fan. Churches and funeral homes routinely distributed similar fans in the early 1900s to help create a breeze. I once viewed a collection of antique funeral home fans that had survived the advent of central air conditioning. Some were made out of cardboard, some of rattan, and all bore the mortuary name on the reverse side. Church fans were a little more economical, always made of cardboard, trumpeting the name of whatever local merchant paid for them.

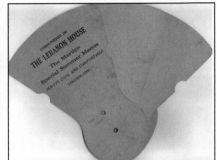

The Marilyn fan

Both types of fans had one thing in common: an inexpensive affixed handle made out of either wood or bamboo. But our fan was different. Made in three sections with a grommet at the bottom, it could be folded up and slipped into a purse or jacket pocket, or fanned out to produce a breeze on a hot summer day. It was made of heavyweight cardboard with a florid, full color pattern on the reverse. On the obverse side was the mystery. The advertising said:

The Lebanon House
Featuring The Summer Marilyn Menus

The name Lebanon House dated the fan from the early to the late 1930s. No great surprise there. Lebanon House was the popular name for the Golden Lamb when Robert Jones bought the hotel in 1926. But who or what was "Marilyn"? I flipped through the scrapbooks in which

Robert and Virginia Jones had meticulously preserved magazine articles and news stories about the hotel, some dating back to the '30s and '40s. I searched old files left behind when the Joneses gave up active management in 1969. I came away with nothing. Eventually, I gave up, put the fan away, and more or less forgot about it. But a few years later, the mystery of "Marilyn" resurfaced.

In the spring of 1993, good friend and local resident Ginny Kuntz was having lunch at the hotel. On the way to her table in the Dickens Room, she asked me to stop over, as there was someone "I just had to meet." Enter Laura Farbach, a former Lebanon resident now living in Cincinnati. At the time I met her, Laura was an alert woman in her 80s who had lots of stories to tell. She had lived in Lebanon during the 1920s and '30s and helped her mother run a restaurant on east Mulberry Street, one block north of the Golden Lamb. Apparently her mother's restaurant was a favorite of local residents for a quick lunch or dinner. "Good food" prepared by a "great cook" were the drawing cards of the business. Business got even better, Laura said, when the restaurant moved around the corner on Broadway.

"Where were you on Broadway?" I asked.

She looked at me as if I had just asked the dumbest question she ever heard. And she was probably right.

Laura glanced around the Dickens Room and said, "Why, we

moved here to the Golden Lamb. Mr. Jones convinced my mother to relocate, because he didn't have a proper restaurant when he bought the place. So we relocated the Marilyn down here."

Well . . . the proverbial light bulb went off over my head. I remembered the fan given to me years earlier and the reference to "Marilyn," and as Laura continued to reminisce, a lot of blanks began to be filled in.

When Bob Jones purchased the Golden Lamb in 1926, the food service was minimal, if not non-existent. He struggled for a few years before finally persuading Laura's mother, "Marilyn" Keoh, to move her restaurant from its Mulberry Street location to the hotel.

Laura pointed behind us to a single door facing Broadway, used as a handicapped entrance. "Mr. Jones had that door put in so people coming to the restaurant didn't have to walk through the hotel lobby." She then pointed to the entrance from the lobby to the dining room. "There were double doors that closed this room off," she explained. "The lunch crowd always got a little noisy, and Mr. Jones wanted to protect the hotel guests from the confusion." I remembered those doors being there when I started at the hotel in 1966. At some point in time, they had been removed to allow for easier access to the dining room and more space in the lobby.

Laura directed our attention to the wine rack in the Dickens Room.

The rack was inset in the wall, but not permanently affixed. We had taken it out several times over the years to re-paint the room. "The original cashier's stand was where the wine rack is," she said. "The same cashier who handled the hotel guests also could cash out the restaurant guests. Guests paid for their food in here instead of the hotel lobby."

She also described the restaurant soda fountain, which ran along the north wall and had a marble counter and tall stools. That revelation explained the solid marble top tables used in the Dickens Room for so many years. They were leftovers from the Marilyn restaurant. These beautiful, old relics got relegated to the hotel dumpster when new tables were purchased in 2003.

Marilyn Keoh apparently insisted on bringing her own staff when she made the move from Mulberry Street, including a young man named Norman Sims. When I started working at the Golden Lamb in the fall of 1966, Chef Norman Sims ruled the hotel's kitchen with an iron hand wrapped in a velvet glove. Gruff and demanding on the outside, "Norm" treated everyone like they were extended family. He regularly served meals to less fortunate individuals, allowing them to sit at his makeshift desk in the rear of the kitchen. The price was always whatever these folks could afford to pay—maybe a dollar, maybe nothing.

Many a night after work, I would pile in the car with a group of other busboys, heading off to a drive-in movie with a meal of Norm's fried chicken packed in a brown paper bag and large, generous slices of German chocolate cake. He always insisted that our carry-out bag be left open, never closed. "Don't close the bag," he would say. "Makes the chicken greasy. And don't ever wrap my fried chicken in aluminum foil." More often than not, the fried chicken never made it to the drive-in. Once the aroma filled the car, even with the windows down, it was impossible to resist. The only thing Norm Sims made better than fried chicken was stuffed peppers. Unfortunately, those didn't travel too well in a moving car.

Laura recalled the disastrous 1928 fire and how her mother had re-opened the dining room within an hour after the firemen left. And she made reference to the "formal dining room," now the Lebanon Room, and the red piano, which always sat just inside the door. It was obvious she had many more stories, but with the mystery of "Marilyn" solved, I left Laura and my friend Ginny Kuntz sitting in the Dickens Room, making a mental note to myself to invite her back to the hotel to fill in more blanks about the Golden Lamb in the 1930s. A few months later, I ran into Ginny again and thanked her for introducing me to such a wealth of information as Laura Farbach. When I told Ginny that I wanted to invite Laura to another lunch—this one longer, so I could record all the stories—she looked grim. "Fred, we're too late. Laura had a stroke two weeks ago and lost the use of her right side and her speech. She's in the hospital now and probably will never leave."

Unfortunately, Laura never did recover and died a few weeks later. There's a lesson here for all historians, one that I learned the hard way. Never pass up a chance to gather information from the Laura Farbachs of the world. I began this book by saying I spent thirty years working the same street corner and listening to anyone who had a story to tell about the Golden Lamb. Unfortunately, in this instance, I didn't listen long enough.

The Golden Lamb today

no...we keep the explosives
on the third floor.
A few words about current history

Most people can't conceive of history being made in their
lifetime. History is something that happened 200 years ago. You read
about it in a book.

Nothing could be further from the truth. History is being made all
around us, every minute of every day. Think for a moment about the
historic events in your own lifetime. Whether you're 75 or 25, your list
should be lengthy. Mine includes the first man to go into outer space,
the first man to walk on the moon, the first president and first vice-
president to resign from office, the first president to be impeached on
live television, the construction (and destruction) of the Berlin Wall,
the first views of modern China . . .

Where, you ask, is this discussion leading? Instead of talking about
Charles Dickens, Henry Clay, and those dead presidents, this chapter
will be devoted to more recent visitors, celebrities and dignitaries who

183

spent some time under the sign of the Golden Lamb. All are famous; one or two are infamous. Some may get their names on doors; some won't. Each person, though, is interesting in his or her own way, and their visits were certainly not without incident.

The first celebrity I ever saw at the Golden Lamb didn't want to be famous. In fact, he was infamous. One court of law said he deserved his infamy. Years later, another said he didn't. Who was right or who was wrong is not for me to decide. All I know is, when this person dropped into the Golden Lamb for dinner, it caused quite a stir.

Samuel Reese Sheppard, or "Dr. Sam" as he became known in the press, was a notorious figure not only in Ohio but across the nation in the late 1950s and early 1960s. Sheppard was an osteopath in Cleveland, Ohio, in 1956 when he was arrested, tried, and convicted of murdering his pregnant wife by bludgeoning her to death with a hammer. The crime's gory details are readily available for anyone who wants to look them up, but they serve no purpose here. Dr. Sam's side of the story was that he came home after a late night at the hospital and saw a mysterious "bushy-haired man" running from the house. Upon investigation, he found his wife dead in their bedroom. (If the story sounds familiar, it's because the same narrative was used in the TV series, *The Fugitive*, and in the 1993 feature film starring Harrison Ford.)

Dr. Sam was a guest in the Ohio Penitentiary from 1954 until 1965, when his appeal reached the U.S. Supreme Court. The high court didn't decide on his guilt or innocence, but ruled that there was enough pre-trial publicity to influence the jury and that Sheppard should get another turn at bat. In his second trial, he had the services of a brash, arrogant, unknown attorney from Houston, Texas, named F. Lee Bailey. It was Bailey's first big case, and he was out to make a name for himself. He argued that Sheppard was the victim of judicial prejudice, jury tampering, and evidence irregularities in his first trial. This time, Dr. Sam was found innocent, and he walked out of court into history.

I had followed the case closely. Liberal young Democrat that I was, I thought justice had finally been served. Here was a man, falsely accused, improperly tried, wrongly imprisoned and now, just like in the movies, a knight comes riding in on a white horse (or, in Bailey's case, a black Lincoln convertible) and wins his freedom.

Shortly after Sheppard's acquittal, I was working at the hotel on a Friday night. Glancing around the Lebanon Room, who should I see but the man himself. Sitting beside him was his girlfriend, a very tall, very blond, German woman named Ariane Tebbenjohanns. (They met while he was in prison. Tebbenjohanns had become a Dr. Sam "groupie," if you will, shortly after Sheppard traded in his Cleveland suburban home for a 10 x 10 prison cell.)

Joining the couple at their table was the still brash, still arrogant, and now very famous F. Lee Bailey. Needless to say, I was impressed. Three people I'd seen on TV, and read about in newspapers and magazines, were sitting in the same room with me. Except I'm not sitting. I'm bussing tables.

I turned to the waitress working next to me, a wonderful woman named Irene Dawson, and whispered, "Look, back on table 21, do you see who that is?"

Irene peered toward the back of the room. "Yeah, who is that?" she asked. "He looks familiar."

"That's Sam Sheppard. You know, Dr. Sam from Cleveland."

Then in a voice loud enough to be heard on the third floor of the hotel, Irene blurted out, "THE GUY WHO MURDERED HIS WIFE?"

Every neck in the room snapped toward us, then to the back of the room. Dr. Sam had been made.

"He didn't murder his wife," I whispered. "He got a new trial and was found innocent."

"Well, sure," Irene said. "The court let him off, but I still don't believe it."

After this brief exchange, we went on about our business until about five minutes later when I notice Dr. Sam looking around the dining room, trying to get the attention of a server. I also notice he has no water, no butter on the table, and no menus. Although there are a lot more employees in this dining room than actually belong here and even some heads peeking out from the kitchen, no one has had the nerve to approach Sheppard and his party. And Dr. Sam is still waiting on his water.

About this time, manager Mary Talcott comes into the room, sees the confusion, then says to me, "What's going on?"

"Look," I whisper, nodding in Dr. Sam's direction. "See who that is?"

Mary has much the same reaction as Irene.

"I've seen him before on television or something," she says. "Who is it?"

Again, I whisper, "That's Sam Sheppard from Cleveland. You know, Dr. Sam."

"THE GUY WHO MURDERED HIS WIFE?"

Again, every neck in the room snaps around to stare at the man.

"He didn't murder his wife," I say firmly. "He was acquitted."

"Sure," Mary replies. "That's what the court said. But I read all that stuff in the paper, and I still think he did it."

Meanwhile, Dr. Sam still has no water.

Mary finally had to go into another dining room and bring back one of the hotel's venerable servers, Millie Benner, who obviously had no feelings one way or the other toward Dr. Sam. The fact that he might or might not have bashed his wife's head in with a ball-peen hammer made no difference to Millie. As long as he left a 15 percent tip, he was innocent until proven guilty.

Dr. Sam was the first, but certainly not the last celebrity guest I met at the hotel. For the most part, the famous and the infamous were pretty nice people, but a few whisked in the door with that "Don't you know who I am?" attitude and made more enemies than friends during the course of a two-hour dinner. My purpose, however, is not to dish dirt but to recount history, so I'll leave the Hollywood horror stories for another book. Instead, let's turn our attention to another group of celebrities who helped make the Golden Lamb what it is today. For where would the hotel be without politicians?

Every time a major political figure visited us, I would say to myself, "Things must have been a lot easier when Ulysses S. Grant came to town." Lay in a good supply of whiskey, a box of cigars, and a comfortable chair, and Grant was probably a happy man. But things have changed. Today, with news cameras recording their every move and sound bites airing a dozen times a day on as many newscasts, politicians have to be careful. Security also is tight, whether it's for a visit by the governor or a whirlwind tour of a presidential candidate.

President's Dining Room

One thing is certain. Whenever a big-name politician blows into town, everybody, and I mean everybody, wants to get in on the act.

In 1968, the local Republican Party snagged Ronald Reagan. The California governor was campaigning across the state on behalf of Ohio candidates on a national level. Remember that last statement, " . . . on a national level." There will be a quiz later.

Reagan was scheduled to speak in the Black Horse Tavern, then located on the lower level of the Golden Lamb. The day of his speech, the place was packed with every political hanger-on in town. The local GOP had fired up its political machine and organized a great turnout for the governor. Being the most Republican city in the most Republican county in the state of Ohio, if a bomb had gone off in the bar that day the Democrats would have been in power for the next 100 years. Come to think of it, there were more than a few Democrats there, too.

From the many conversations going on around me, I gathered that the substance of Reagan's speech was of little importance to those in attendance. They didn't take off work in the middle of the week and get dressed in a suit . . . for politics. People were there to see Ronald Reagan the actor, not Ronald Reagan the governor of California. At the appointed hour, a crowd formed outside the tavern door as Reagan's motorcade pulled up. Suddenly the door swung open and there he was: Ronald Reagan, of *Death Valley Days* . . . Ronald Reagan, of *G.E. Theater* . . . Ronald Reagan, of *Knute Rockne, All American* . . . And, oh yeah, Ronald Reagan, governor of California. (If you're under 40, ask your parents about *Death Valley Days* and *G.E. Theater*. If you're under 25, ask your grandparents.)

Reagan looked much the same as he would when he became our president in the 1980s. The hair was neatly-coiffed and dark. He sported a great tan. He wore a crisp summer suit without a speck of dust or a wrinkle, despite a day of traveling throughout the state. The shirt was so white, it almost hurt your eyes to look at it, and he had a beautiful silk tie. Why his tie impressed me so much, I have no idea. Maybe it was because I had to wear a black bow-tie every day for the first four years of my working life.

Reagan swept through the door and started working the room. Nobody, and I mean nobody, got more than thirty seconds with the man, but everybody walked away with the feeling that "I talked with Ronald Reagan." The future president of the United States pressed the local flesh for about twenty minutes, then walked up to the microphone and began to speak. And as luck would have it, the microphone was dead. So here were a couple of hundred fired-up Republicans, drooling on their checkbooks, waiting to contribute, and the star attraction couldn't be heard. But this was Ronald Reagan, "The Great Communicator." The governor pointed and said, "Get me that chair. I'll stand on a chair and make my speech."

Reagan hopped up on one of our big Windsor chairs in the tavern and began to speak. All eyes were on him, except for mine. Having watched the chair being put in place, my eyes were on Reagan's feet. The suave and dapper governor of California, the future president of the United States, was wearing scuffed up, muddy cowboy boots. I'm not even talking good-looking boots. I'm talking two-toned leather, curly-que stitching cowboy boots. They were dusty, too.

But that's not the punch line to the story. Remember, I mentioned that Reagan was campaigning on behalf of Ohio candidates "on a national level." And remember, I said there was going to be a quiz? Reagan stood on a chair in the basement of the Golden Lamb in '68 and made a glowing, eloquent speech on behalf of an Ohio congressman he described as "the heart of the Republican Party and the hope of the future." Ok, here's the question: who was standing beside Ronald Reagan as the recipient of all that praise and glowing oratory? Well, the "heart of the Republican Party" and the "hope of the future" was none other than local Congressman Donald E. "Buzz" Lukens.

For those of you unfamiliar with Ohio politics in the '70s and '80s, let me put it this way. In the late 1990s, the nation learned of the alleged dalliances of President Bill Clinton in a political drama that played out on national television. Ten years earlier, on a smaller scale, Ohioans were treated to a daily dose of the Buzz Lukens scandals. Congressman Buzz, born in nearby Harveysburg, Ohio, was censured in Congress for an alleged affair with a 16-year-old girl. (The young lady allegedly had the foresight to bring along a tape recorder on several of their "dates." She may have been a teenager, but she wasn't dumb.) A short time later, Lukens was kicked out of the U.S. House of Representatives for "allegedly" sexually harassing the Capitol's female elevator operators. Then, after the 1995 investigation of a House banking scandal, Buzz was hauled into court to face charges of allegedly peddling influence during his latter years in Congress. He presented, I feel, a very plausible defense. By the end of his career in politics, Buzz argued, "I had no influence left. Nobody paid attention to what I said." Unfortunately, the courts didn't buy it, and Buzz was convicted.

In 1976, eight years after Reagan's stump (er, chair) speech, another big politico breezed into Lebanon to campaign, this time on his own behalf. Once again, the local Republicans hooked a major player who just happened to be running for the office of vice president of the United States. As a means of introduction to this story, let me ask the question: What were you doing August 8, 1974, at approximately nine o'clock in the evening? (Anyone over the age of 40 should have no trouble remembering. This event certainly fits into the category of current history.)

If you were like most Americans, you were sitting in front of your TV, witnessing an unprecedented event in American history. A sitting president of the United States was about to resign from office. In the wake of the Watergate scandal, Richard Milhous Nixon, our 38th chief executive, was finally going to call it quits and let somebody else take the heat, all from the safety and serenity of his private San Clemente, California estate.

Following Nixon's resignation, Vice President Gerald Ford got the keys to Air Force One. As you may remember, Ford had become vice president after Nixon's running mate, Spiro Agnew, went on TV and made "nolo contendre" a household word. Ford cruised along on autopilot as president for about eighteen months until suddenly it came time to run for office. Nelson Rockefeller, who had been appointed vice president, politely said, "Been there, done that," when asked to accompany Ford on the Republican ticket. So, when the GOP began searching for a running mate for Gerald Ford, the party used the "3-M" test. The candidate had to be Male . . . had to have Money . . . and had to be from the Midwest.

Bob Dole, a United States senator from Kansas, fit the bill. The fact that Dole was a war hero was just icing on the cake. The plan was for Senator Dole to make an old-fashioned whistle stop tour through Ohio, but because train travel was long gone in the state, this tour would be by bus. And of course the bus would make a stop in historic Lebanon.

Hotel manager Jack Reynolds and I had about ten days' advance notice of Dole's visit, and we hastily started making plans. Being a good southern Democrat, Jack knew the president and the senator didn't have a snowball's chance of winning the election, but stranger things have happened. Maybe the Ford-Dole ticket could pull it off and we might have another name to add to our impressive list of presidential visitors.

The itinerary was simple. Dole would make a speech at the Warren County Historical Society, just two doors south of the Golden Lamb. Once the speech was over, the Kansas senator would walk up to the hotel for an hour of what the Secret Service jokingly called "grip and grin shots." In other words, anyone who contributed enough money to the campaign could have his or her photograph taken shaking hands with the candidate. The photo would look impressive on a mantle or behind a desk.

Thus, all the Ford-Dole campaign wanted was a place to take photographs. Jack and I thought the Presidents Room on the second floor would be the best location. It had lots of space, easy access, and was full of portraits of all those august nineteenth century and early twentieth century U.S. presidents who visited the Golden Lamb. It was a no-brainer.

We had everything mapped out and under control until the Secret Service arrived. I should add that this was my first experience working with this federal law enforcement agency—an experience I'm not likely ever to forget. Writing about it now, the whole episode is just as vivid and just as frustrating as if it happened yesterday.

Several agents came to town a few days ahead of Dole's arrival, and after working with them I began to ask myself the same question over and over again: "What's so secret about the Secret Service?" They all looked alike in their three-piece polyester suits, regulation haircuts, sideburns down to the bottom of the earlobe, and a bulge under the left arm where each packed a gun. And they were cheap. One agent came down to breakfast, purchased a copy of the *Cincinnati Enquirer* (25 cents), and asked for a receipt. Another ordered a hamburger for lunch and upon discovering it was 15 cents extra for cheese, decided he was getting too much dairy in his diet anyway.

The Secret Service immediately scrapped our plans for the senator's appearance. The second-floor Presidents Room "just wouldn't do" because of its lack of windows. Protecting the candidate would be too difficult unless he could be viewed from the outside. I assumed that security for Dole would be a snap; at that time not many people knew what the guy looked like anyway. And remember, he was fronting for a party in disgrace. Neither Dole nor Ford was getting a lot of photo ops with the press.

Nevertheless, it was decided that the Buckeye Room on the ground floor would be more suitable. Every piece of furniture was removed, with the exception of a single painting on the wall, a small couch, and a coffee table commandeered from Jack Reynolds's living room. The party faithful were to form a line to the left, then each patiently wait for his or her turn to "grip and grin" with Dole, who would be positioned in front of the painting and standing between the coffee table and couch. Imagine school "Picture Day" . . . but with a lot more guns.

The day of the event we received a "briefing" by the Secret Service, who informed us, "Just stay out of the way, and everything will be fine." Then it was time for "show and tell." The agent in charge introduced us to all of the agents participating in the day's activities. (Again, after about five minutes I began asking myself, "What's so secret about the Secret Service?")

"Now this agent is wearing a white lapel pin with a red circle around the outside. He's a member of the bomb squad.

"This agent is wearing a white lapel pin with a green band around the outside. He's with communications.

"This agent is wearing a red lapel pin with a blue band around the outside. He's a member of Senator Dole's personal detail."

"And this agent . . ."

Half an hour later, I saw a guy walking through the lobby wearing a gold lapel pin with a blue band. Pointing to his pin, I asked, "What part of the Secret Service are you with?" He gave me a rather strange look and told me he was a Rotarian.

Managers also were assigned their own personal Secret Service agents, just in case Jack or I tried to assassinate a politician neither of us had ever seen before. I'll never forget my agent. His name was Harry.

Ten minutes before Dole was to walk through the door of the

Golden Lamb, my guy Harry stomps his foot on the floor and says, "What's underneath here?"

"A basement," I said.

"What do you keep down there?"

"China . . . glassware . . . paper supplies . . . you know, restaurant stuff," I said.

"Keep any explosives down there?" Harry asked.

I wanted to say, "No Harry, we keep the explosives on the third floor," but I didn't. I assured him there were no propane tanks, fuel oil tanks, or large quantities of flammable liquids stored one floor beneath our feet.

"Well, let's you and me just check it out," Harry said, drawing out the sentence as if to imply, "Don't mess with me, history boy."

I dutifully led Harry back through the dining room, into the kitchen, and down the old concrete steps to the basement. I paused before the doorway to the basement, took a deep breath, and then turned on the light.

(We're going to pause here for a minute. We'll return to the story, I promise. We're stopping so I can tell you that I am about to lead an agent of the United States Secret Service into a basement dating back to 1815. The Golden Lamb building underwent major additions in the nineteenth century, as well as a couple more additions in the last century, each of which added more basement space.

The basement has brick foundations, stone foundations, some poured concrete foundations, you name it. It extends from one end of the building to the other, with lots of little cut-outs and tunnels leading to various storage areas. If you're familiar with the building, imagine yourself at the front desk waiting to pay your check. Directly in front of you is a pair of half doors that lead to a set of stairs. You can take those stairs down to the basement, wind your way through to the back of the building a half a block away, and never be above ground.

Remember, I told Harry we kept china, glassware, paper supplies, and restaurant stuff in the basement. Well, I probably should have clarified the "stuff." At that time, the Golden Lamb had old equipment, light bulbs, broken chairs, china, unopened boxes of glassware, old opened boxes of glassware, maintenance supplies, candles, flower vases, old checks and other "stuff" that hadn't been moved in forty years.

To give you a more visual picture, imagine what your own living room looks like about five minutes after your kids get done opening all of their Christmas presents. There was crap everywhere. And this was what Harry and I were about to "check out.")

OK . . . back to the story. Harry and I are at the entrance to the basement. I turned on the light, and the first words out of

Harry's mouth were unpublishable. Let's just say he expressed some displeasure at the task before him. He looked at me. I looked at him and shrugged my shoulders.

"We should have gotten in here days ago," said Harry as he began his search. He walked around the first room of the basement, looking in a barrel here, peering inside a half-empty box there, wondering how to search an entire floor-to-ceiling wall of paint cans. Harry was particularly intrigued by a dark crawl space in the wall directly behind a large grease trap in the middle of the basement.

"Where does that go to?" he asked.

"Nobody knows," I said.

"Oh," Harry replied, indicating he wasn't going to be the first one to find out.

After a few minutes of touring numerous dark, damp, low-ceiling rooms full of virtually everything that could have been used in a restaurant in the last fifty years, Harry looked me dead in the eye and asked the dumbest question I'd ever heard in my life.

"Does anything look out of place?"

After I stopped laughing, I told Harry everything was "out of place," but typical of a 175-year-old building. We backtracked through the basement, up the stairs, and through the kitchen with Harry looking down at the ground and shaking his head the whole time.

Fortunately, no bombs were planted downstairs and Senator Dole spent an hour grippin' and grinnin', walking away with a pocketful of checks.

Despite the healthy contributions from the local party faithful, Bob Dole would watch the inauguration from the audience. Jimmy Carter was sworn in as president, with Walter Mondale as vice president. Mondale, the two-term U.S. senator from Minnesota, had successfully passed the 3-M test with Democrats. Dole would return to Lebanon several decades later during his run for the presidency. This time, there was no gripping and grinning, just campaign buses parked in the middle of the street and the good senator on a bullhorn. Dole lost again. Who says history doesn't repeat itself?

In 1988, another presidential hopeful visited the Golden Lamb. Actually the candidate stayed behind and sent his wife out to do the gripping and grinning. Barbara Bush, wife of then-Vice President George Bush, made a visit to beat the "bushes," so to speak, and shake loose a little money for her husband's campaign. Once again the party faithful turned out in droves, and once again the Secret Service was on hand. But I'm getting ahead of myself. The chaos and confusion started a whole lot earlier.

A couple of months before Mrs. Bush's visit, I returned to work after a rare three days off in a row. I never particularly liked having two days off in a row, let alone three. So much goes on in the space of seventy-two hours, and I felt it took me a full day just to catch up. That particular morning, I grabbed a handful of messages taped to the old switchboard and asked our reservationist, Elaine Dulovich, what had gone on in the past three days.

"Not too exciting," Elaine said. "We had a couple of hundred for lunch on Tuesday, same on Wednesday. We got killed on Tuesday night . . . only ninety-eight people."

I was halfway down the steps to my office when I heard her say, "Oh, by the way, Barbara Bush called. She booked four rooms for the first week in May."

I took about three more steps before the words hit me, then came back up the stairs.

"*The* Barbara Bush?" I asked. "Washington D.C. Barbara Bush? Mrs. Vice President of the United States Barbara Bush?"

"Yeah, that's the one," said Elaine. "And let me tell you, I had a heck of a time getting a credit card guarantee for the rooms."

I was incredulous. "You asked the wife of the vice president of the United States for her credit card number? How could you do that?"

"Well, it wasn't her, it was her secretary," Elaine explained. "Besides, I plan on voting for [Michael] Dukakis."

Within a few days, details of Mrs. Bush's visit began to filter in.

She would be on (what else?) a fund-raising swing through Ohio, with appearances in Cincinnati, Lebanon, and then on to Middletown. She would arrive at the hotel late in the evening on a Tuesday, with a breakfast reception the following morning. So now we were faced with the daunting task of preparing for an overnight visit, not your typical barnstorming stop. Mrs. Bush and her entourage (and I use that in the truest sense of the word) would be bunking down at "Ohio's Oldest Inn," and the GOP expected us to put on a show.

Jack and I decided on Room 27 for Mrs. Bush. The third-floor room was the largest in the Golden Lamb, with two double beds and a single, and it also was scheduled to be redecorated in a few months. Needless to say, the re-decoration began immediately. New wallpaper, paint, curtains and carpet were ordered, and guests were shuffled to make way for "Barb." The entire project took only about a week, with Jack figuratively sitting on the work crews to get the renovations done. All was in readiness about a week prior to Mrs. Bush's visit.

We shouldn't have bothered.

As soon as the Secret Service arrived, they systematically changed all our plans. Room 27 on the third floor "just wouldn't do," for Mrs. Bush. The room we had picked out for Bob Dole didn't have enough windows. This room, however, had too many windows. Also, the flat roof just outside the south wall of the room made protecting Mrs. Bush "an impossibility." By the time the Secret Service was done, Mrs. Bush was to spend the night in the McKinley Room on the second floor and the original four rooms had now grown to twelve. This was your tax dollars at work, folks, so let me run it down for you.

One room was for Mrs. Bush. One room was for her secretary. That makes two.

We could not rent the rooms on either side of Mrs. Bush. We could not rent the two rooms directly above Mrs. Bush. That makes six.

The Secret Service had to have a separate room for their "command post." That makes seven. (In case you're ever asked to set up a command post for the Secret Service, it's nothing more than an empty room with a dedicated telephone line. But because the government was paying full double rate, what did I care?)

Secret Service also had to have a room where the agents could "relax." I didn't understand how agents had time to kick back, but their "relaxing" room was an extra large double with a premium rate, so let them sleep the night away. By the way, that makes EIGHT rooms.

Various staff and other hangers-on occupied the other four rooms. The importance of political staff can be gauged by their accessories. Anybody with a briefcase is probably brand-new and just trying to look important, but they're really not. The only accessory more telling than a briefcase is a day planner. Any staff member who openly displayed a day planner is about as far down on the political food chain as you can get. Clipboards were about one step up the organizational chain from a briefcase. The real power always lies with the person carrying "the notebook." Most really important people I've met at the Golden Lamb carry their lives in a three-ring binder that is constantly updated. Lose the notebook and the game is over.

Mrs. Bush carried the notebook. Despite my then-Democratic leanings, I had to admire the lady for taking charge of her own details. She spent a very uneventful night at the Golden Lamb, which is more than can be said for some of our other guests. We had more than a few calls from overnight guests asking about the guys in dark suits roaming the halls all night and talking into their sleeves.

The next morning, the party faithful gathered down the hall in the Presidents Room, checkbooks in hand (or at least readily available), to drink overpriced coffee, eat overpriced Danish and wait for the chance to "grip and grin" with Barb. Meanwhile, outside the building, a small army of law enforcement officials gathered to form a motorcade for the trip to Middletown.

Remember, I said when a major political figure comes to town, everybody wants to get in on the act? Well, with the wife of the sitting vice president visiting Lebanon, no one was going to be left out. The limousine that would take Mrs. Bush to Middletown was parked directly in front of the hotel. Directly in front and in back of the limo were police cruisers from the city of Middletown. In front and in back of the Middletown cruisers were Ohio Highway Patrol vehicles. Directly in front and in back of the state patrol cars were Warren County sheriff's cruisers. Directly in front and in back of the sheriff's cruisers were cars from the Lebanon Police Department. I can only assume as each car lost its jurisdiction, it would peel away, leaving Mrs. Bush high and dry by the time she got to the Manchester Hotel in Middletown. I'm also sure that if the fire department and the parks department could have wormed their way in, the parade would have been even longer.

Mrs. Bush proved to be a warm and cordial guest. She publicly vowed that if her husband were elected (notice she said if and not when), she would definitely bring him back to Lebanon because of the wonderful reception she had received. Well, George made it to the White House, but as of this writing has yet to make it to Lebanon. I assume the hotel would still welcome him. John Quincy Adams wasn't president when he was here and neither was Harding, but the hotel still milks their historical significance for all it's worth. So George, the welcome mat is still out.

If Mrs. Bush makes good on her promise and one day brings her husband back to Lebanon, I can only hope for one thing. Please let me be out of town.

rising from the ashes
now a modern hotel

There's one piece I've always admired that lies outside the walls of "Ohio's Oldest Inn." Most guests pass right by it, eager to get to their tables or the gift shop, or to check in to the hotel. How it got where it is, and why, requires one last story.

In March of 1936, Bob and Virginia Jones stood on the sidewalk and watched in horror as flames engulfed the fourth floor of their hotel. Their first thoughts were probably not of a bricks-and-mortar building being destroyed, but of a tradition about to die a fiery death. The old Golden Lamb stood on the corner of Main and Broadway for well over a hundred years, and now it was in danger of being lost forever. The historic hotel that had accommodated Henry Clay, Daniel Webster, Charles Dickens and ten U.S. presidents, among other notable figures, was going up in flames.

Later that day, with the fire extinguished and the water still dripping down from the fourth floor, Bob Jones re-opened for business, vowing to keep the tradition alive. He would hire architect Albert

Mr. and Mrs. Jones

Harmon and announce ambitious plans to rebuild the old landmark hotel, bigger and better than ever. After the renovation, Jones had a sign made to hang underneath the new balcony, just outside the front door. Made of cast iron, the sign was sure to survive, no matter what ravages might befall the old hotel in the future. It would be a permanent marker, reminding future generations of the Golden Lamb's rich history and traditions.

So . . . the next time you exit the hotel's front door, before you rush off to Lebanon's newest antique shop or walk to your car, take a few seconds and look up. Take the time to read Bob Jones's proud, if somewhat ironic, declaration made in 1937: *Famous since 1815 as the "Golden Lamb" and the oldest Inn still operating as a hotel in Ohio. Here J.Q. Adams, Henry Clay, Chas. Dickens and many other famous men have stayed. Now a modern hotel.* It ain't modern and hopefully never will be. Seventy years after Bob Jones hung that sign, the Golden Lamb still faithfully maintains a tradition of nineteenth century hospitality and preservation of nineteenth century American life.

Photo Credits

Cremmins Painting of Dickens Collection-The Golden Lamb Collection

Drawing of Charles Dickens-Author's Collection

Dickens Dinner Menu-Author's Collection

Regina Music Box-Tom Cloud/Silver Cloud Productions

Coachman's Bench-Tom Cloud/Silver Cloud Productions

Shaker Chest-Tom Cloud/Silver Cloud Productions

Photo of Golden Lamb Early 1900s-Author's Collection

Drawing of Henry Clay Room-The Golden Lamb Collection

Lew Hudnall Painting-The Golden Lamb Collection

Joe Emmet Christmas Card-The Golden Lamb Collection

Bobby Taylor Painting-The Golden Lamb Collection

Early Dessert Menu-Author's Collection

Dickens of A Christmas Menu-Author's Collection

1940's Card-Author's Collection

Dickens' Bootleg Books-Tom Cloud/Silver Cloud Productions

Ale Warmer-Tom Cloud/Silver Cloud Productions

Ink Wells-Tom Cloud/Silver Cloud Productions

Cremmins Painting of The Golden Lamb-The Golden Lamb Collection

Early Christmas Card By Nancy Bassford-The Golden Lamb Collection

Kitchen Staff 1940s- The Portman Family

Golden Lamb Photo 1940-50-The Portman Family

Corwin Room Drawing-The Golden Lamb Collection

Formal Dining Room Photo-The Portman Family

Vallandigham Room Drawing-The Golden Lamb Collection

Killer Bed-Tom Cloud/Silver Cloud Productions

Dickens Bed-Tom Cloud/Silver Cloud Productions

Dickens Bed, Fred Compton-Tom Cloud/Silver Cloud Productions

Our Last Christmas Card-The Golden Lamb Collection

Drawing of Presidents Dining Room-The Golden Lamb Collection

Photo of Mr. and Mrs. Robert Jones-Warren County History Center